AMERICAN ANTI-WAR MOVEMENTS

The Insight Series
Studies in Contemporary Issues
from The Glencoe Press

PROBLEMS OF AMERICAN FOREIGN POLICY
Martin B. Hickman

THE OPPENHEIMER AFFAIR:
a political play in three acts
Joseph Boskin and Fred Krinsky

THE POLITICS OF RELIGION IN AMERICA
Fred Krinsky

THE WELFARE STATE:
who is my brother's keeper?
Fred Krinsky and Joseph Boskin

OPPOSITION POLITICS:
the anti-new deal tradition
Joseph Boskin

IS AMERICAN DEMOCRACY EXPORTABLE?
Edward G. McGrath

PROTEST FROM THE RIGHT
Robert A. Rosenstone

DEMOCRACY AND COMPLEXITY:
who governs the governors?
Fred Krinsky

FERMENT IN LABOR
Jerome Wolf

AMERICAN ANTI-WAR MOVEMENTS
Joseph Conlin

URBAN VIOLENCE
Joseph Boskin

Series Editors: Fred Krinsky and Joseph Boskin

AMERICAN ANTI-WAR MOVEMENTS

Joseph R. Conlin

Assistant Professor
Department of History
Chico State College

THE GLENCOE PRESS
A Division of The Macmillan Company
Beverly Hills
Collier-Macmillan Ltd., London

First printing, 1968.

Library of Congress catalog card number: 68-25164

The Glencoe Press
A Division of The Macmillan Company.

Printed in the United States of America.

Collier-Macmillan Canada, Ltd., Toronto, Canada.

Printed in the United States of America.

Preface

An occasional American has glorified war. Rear Admiral S. B. Luce, for example, wrote in 1891 of the "cankers of a calm world and long peace" and suggested that "but for war, the civilization we now enjoy would have been impossible." At least one president of the nation, Theodore Roosevelt, was titillated by the military way. And popular songs, in recent times, have pictured the soldier as the *beau ideal* of young manhood while politicians suggest turning political decision-making over to generals.

Historically, however, these attitudes are not typically American. Large segments of the population have been vocally critical of all American wars and even larger numbers have been apathetic. The soldier and sailor of tradition was an unsavory professional, a necessary evil perhaps, but one with whom the respectable citizen did not associate. And the Anglo-Saxon distrust of large peacetime armies was, until the late 1940's, an established and revered principle. Americans have been a violent people but, throughout most of their history, they have not loved war.

It is no great puzzle to understand why anyone should hate war. It is, at its most innocuous, disruptive of society. War moreover, means purely and simply wholesale killing and destruction. War meant mass misery five hundred years ago and, in the 1960's, war between major powers assumes a holocaust from which civilization and even *homo sapiens* would emerge unrecognizable if at all. Americans, in addition, have prided themselves on a vague superiority to the corruptions of Europe, not the least of which corruptions was Europe's endemic warfare.

To protest publicly one's love of peace in the United States is a piety as uncontroversial as the condemnation of cannibalism. Citizens may claim to hate war even during wartime if they are quick to add that peace sometimes requires war as a prelude. Thus, priests intone their love of peace as they bless battleships, politicians as they vote military credits, scholars as they devise justifications for attacks, businessmen as they raise their prices, and four-star generals as they do their job. And "the people" applaud all and don their uniforms.

This is the way it has been, and it is not enough to dismiss concurrent American cries for peace and readiness for war as ironical or hypocritical. Americans have been, simply, a people who would prefer peace but are quick, if real or imagined interests are threatened, to find their solution in war.

But "Americans at War" is not the topic of this study. That topic is derived from the fact that the enthusiasm of Americans for their wars has never been unanimous. From the time when the colonies were established some American voices have been raised against war in general and specific wars in particular. Sometimes muted but often strident and occasionally significant, these voices are as much the heritage of the United States as its people's patriotism.

The voices have been diverse. There have been those who opposed all wars, refusing to recognize the traditional distinctions of "just" and "unjust," "aggressive" and "defensive." They have always been a tiny minority; they are the *pacifists*.

At various times, those who have held that men possess the moral right to violence in order to defend themselves or others have opposed the government and the nation over specific wars in which they found their country's cause unwise, unjust, or venal. They were not pacifists opposed to war, but *opponents of wars*.

Still others have frankly or covertly favored the cause of the nation's enemy and set themselves against the nation's war effort on behalf of their cause. They are the *fifth columnists*.

This study is not concerned with those who have preached peace while practicing war. It is concerned with these three groups which have both preached opposition to war and actively pitted themselves against it. The history of each group has usually followed its separate way. Pacifists have generally cooperated with non-pacifist opponents of wars only after grave misgivings, and not at all with those who do not object to the warmaking of America's enemies. Fifth columnists and often non-pacifist opponents of American wars have scorned pacifists as hopeless visionaries. Thus, the three are herein treated separately.

In the decade of the sixties, however, what was impossible has become potentially significant reality. In the movement aimed at ending the American intervention in Vietnam, pacifists who viewed this war as neither better nor worse than any other but simply as barbaric because it was a war; non-pacifists who saw their country's actions as either foolish, unprecedentedly brutal, badly motivated, or dangerous; and young social revolutionaries who frankly hoped for a victory of America's adversary—all somehow came together to cooperate remarkably well in their common goal, the end of the American intervention. This development marks the end of this slim volume but, perhaps, it marks a new key chapter in the history of American anti-war movements.

J.R.C.

Chico, California
April, 1968

(NOTE.—Throughout this book, the author–editors' footnotes are marked by symbols— *, †—and the original quoted notes by numerals.)

CONTENTS

AMERICAN ANTI-WAR MOVEMENTS

Chapter One:

American Pacifists

The Quakers

To Americans, the most familiar pacifists are the Quakers and, indeed, the Quakers are almost entirely an American phenomenon. Not that all Quakers (or "Friends" as they prefer) are Americans; there are Quakers in three dozen countries. But three-fifths of the world's total reside in the United States and it has been in the United States that they have best prospered.

The idea of "Friendly Persuasion" was a product of the religious and social ferment of seventeenth century England. It was the conception of George Fox (1624–1691), a Lancashire villager known as a cobbler whose real vocation was religious mysticism. From his late teens at least, Fox was preoccupied with his relationship to God. He was confused and aggrieved by the age's incessant theological bickering among Papists, Anglicans, Separatists, Puritans and a host of now-forgotten sects such as Adamites and Familists. The pious Fox was especially disturbed by the prominence which the disputants gave external matters such as church structure. Fox was concerned with internal, *personal* religion, and he turned to it to escape the theological chaos of his time.

At about twenty-two years of age, Fox experienced a conversion, discovering that he needed no church of any sort to mediate between himself and his God. He concluded, in fact, that God was within himself and within every man. He and all men needed only to follow this "Inner Light" in order to perfect themselves in the divine image.

From this idea of an Inner Light developed the peculiar ideas for which Quakers were known and persecuted. First, of course, was their rejection of all church structure including not only the hierarchical organization of the Catholics and Anglicans but also the congregational division of the powerful Puritans. If God was within every man, the Friends reasoned, what need was there for an institutionalized church, ponderous volumes of dogma, sacraments, a sophisticated clergy, and so on? Christianity was an inward experience.

Such ideas were calculated to frighten the English establishment. When a group of Puritans had petitioned King James I to abolish the episcopal structure of the Church of England and institute a congregational structure (1603), James had reasoned that to attack hierarchy in religion meant to attack monarchy in government and he threatened to harry the Puritans from the land. How much more threatening to the status quo seemed this far more radical concept of the Friends?

Moreover, their vision of an Inner Light within *all* men led the Quakers to attach new emphasis to the old but neglected Christian idea that all men were equal in the sight of God. Only a very few Friends divined from this that there should be no social distinctions among men. But almost all came to conclusions which seemed quite as revolutionary to the seventeenth century. Friends insisted, for example, on addressing all men (including magistrates, noblemen, and even the King) in the singular *thou, thee,* and *thy* forms rather than the plural *you*. While such speech sounds merely quaint today, the *thou* form was still in use during the seventeenth century and sometimes denoted the social inferiority of the person addressed, *you* being reserved for social superiors. For a humble Quaker to address a nobleman as *thou* (and to refuse to remove his hat) was a gross insult which often earned the Friend a flogging, fine, or term in prison.

Their Friendly Persuasion also led Quakers into the vanguard of philanthropic movements such as prison reform and the abolition of slavery. Their egalitarianism led them to espouse sexual equality and representative government with a devotion rivalling that of any other group. And finally, as every man had a part of God within him, Friends would not take another's life. In recent years members of the Society have led campaigns aimed at abolishing capital punishment. From their beginnings Quakers have refused to take part in war.

The Quakers came to America under most propitious circumstances. A consortium of wealthy Friends briefly held title to what is now New Jersey and the most important Quaker after George Fox, William Penn (1643–1718), accepted as payment of a debt owed his father by King Charles II a grant of land between New York and Maryland.

Penn conceived of his colony in part as a profitmaking enterprise, but also as a "Holy Experiment" in which the Friends could test their visions of "brotherly love." For they were interested not simply in individual salvation. The Quakers viewed man himself as perfectible and, along with man, man's society. Religious strife, they believed, could be ended in a society where all men were free to worship as they pleased. Social conflict would be assuaged by a representative government in which the general citizenry participated. And war could be banished, they thought, by society's refusal to wage it.

From the point of view of the Friends' idealism, Pennsylvania was a failure. This was most conspicuous in relation to their most delicate tenet, their opposition to militarism and war in general. The less friendly greater society demanded compromises from the beginning. William Penn was obligated, in his role as proprietor of Pennsylvania, to accept a commission as Captain-General of the Army.

The Quaker grandees of Philadelphia valiantly attempted to follow their consciences. Seventy years of sporadic warfare between England and France broke out in 1689 and North America was soon a theatre of conflict. Colonial response to the wars was spotty at best. While colonies such as Massachusetts took enthusiastically to the field and sea (they feared the close French presence in Acadia), other colonies virtually ignored fighting in which they felt no concrete stake. During the early stages of the long conflict, Pennsylvania was far removed from the actual fighting and the Quakers were able to toy casually with Parliament's impatient demands for financial contributions. The favorite Quaker ploy was to grant money "for the King's use," a clever if transparent rationalization of their pacifism. (They satisfied themselves that they were not waging war at the same time that they kept within the King's good graces.)

The war came to Pennsylvania itself by midcentury, however, and Quaker pacifism was sorely tried. Euphemistic evasion was no longer possible, for the Friends were torn between their ideals of representative government and of pacifism. By midcentury, the Pennsylvania backcountry was filling up with non-Quakers who were not only not pacifists, they were rough and ready frontiersmen who coveted the lands of the Indians, feared the presence of potentially warlike aborigines in the neighborhood, and sought an active military campaign of conquest, if not of extermination, against them.

What were the Quakers, who controlled the Pennsylvania legislature, to do? To persist in their policy of peace with the Indians was to fly in the face of the clear wishes of the majority of Pennsylvanians. To adhere strictly to their principle of representative government meant to wage a war which mocked their consciences. The old tactic of granting funds "for the King's use" was no longer sufficient. The frontiersmen wanted armed men and active support. Moreover, many strict Quakers already regretted the earlier compromises and insisted that financial support of armies, no matter how cleverly veiled, was as obnoxious to the Friendly Persuasion as the actual bearing of arms.

The Quakers could argue effectively that their pacifism toward the Indians proved a resounding success—for Quakers. "Is it not a consideration worthy of thankful remembrance," wrote Israel Pemberton in 1756, "that in all the desolation in our frontiers . . . we have reason to think [that the Indians] would never hurt Friends if they knew us to be such?"* It was true. With a few ambiguous exceptions, the Indians of Pennsylvania did not molest Quakers throughout the colonial period; stories were told of tribes directing their braves to spare Quaker homes. But the conflict between the Indians and the other frontiersmen was real and bloody and those frontiersmen demanded action.

---

* Quoted in Brent E. Barksdale, *Pacifism and Democracy in Colonial Pennsylvania* ("Stanford Honors Essays in the Humanities," Vol. III [Stanford, Calif.: Stanford University Press, 1961]), p. 27.

The Quakers' solution ignored William Penn's ringing declaration that "true Godliness does not take men out of the world but enables them to live better in it and excites their endeavours to mend it."* For the Quakers decided that in order to preserve their personal ideals and their coveted religious freedom (there were threats that Quaker worship would be proscribed from London if the Friends persisted in resisting the war), they would withdraw from the active governance of the colony. Almost to the man, Quaker officeholders retired from office in 1756 and allowed Pennsylvania to go to war.

Strictly speaking, the Quakers did not sacrifice their pacifism. They continued personally to refuse to participate in any military venture. What they abandoned was the Holy Experiment, a whole society based on the refusal to wage war. It was a singular failure. The times were not ready for a Pennsylvania. Perhaps the times never will be ready for one.

Although specific wartime situations have from time to time produced splinter groups of "Fighting Quakers" (individuals as militaristically inclined as Richard M. Nixon have claimed to be Friends), most members of the Society have continued since 1756 to oppose all war. They have been conspicuous as conscientious objectors in every war the nation has fought and suffered painfully for their principle. A Quaker named Himelius Hockett refused service in the Confederate Army during the Civil War. He was starved for five days while deserters were branded with an iron in his presence. Along with his brother, also a conscientious objector, Hockett was sentenced to six months at hard labor, fastened to a ball and chain, and ordered to work unloading ordnance cars. Hockett's brother refused it as military work and was bayonetted four inches deep while hanging by his thumbs. Another Quaker resister, Seth Loflin (Loughlin), was kept awake for thirty-six hours, then bound and kicked and hung by his thumbs for an hour and a half each day for a week. He was sentenced to be shot but the execution squad refused to fire. To no avail. Loflin died later from resumed torture.†

Conscription was reintroduced during the Spanish-American conflict but that "splendid little war" was over too quickly for Quaker resistance to be noticed. But the depredations committed against them during World War I, when patriotic hysteria far exceeded that of the Civil War, were numerous, atrocious, and, in many cases, condoned in the highest ranks of the military. By the time of World War II, recognized pacifists such as the Quakers were accorded far more humane treatment, although isolated examples of maltreatment of those who refused all cooperation with the military were reported.

The most notable Quaker development in the twentieth century has been a reversal of the retreat of 1756. Quakers, of course, are no longer in a position to direct the state of Pennsylvania to abstain from American wars. But the Friends have increasingly begun to regard pacifism as more than a matter of personal conscientious objection. More frequent wars and more destructive weapons have emphasized to them the urgency of their pacifism. Quakers have

---

* William Penn, "No Cross, No Crown" (pamphlet; London: 1669).

† John Sykes, *The Quakers* (New York: J. B. Lippincott Co., 1959), p. 87.

renewed the spirit of the Holy Experiment by taking to the streets in demonstration, agitating directly for a more peaceful American foreign policy in particular and a future of peace in general.

Other Religious Pacifist Groups

The Quakers are not the only Christian sect in the United States which has maintained a consistent opposition to war. Colonial Pennsylvania's antimilitarism and promise of religious toleration attracted thousands of Palatine Germans* whose pietistic views closely resembled those of the Friends and who had been beleaguered by war and harassment in their homeland. These thrifty Amish and Mennonites moved beyond Philadelphia to what became Lancaster and York counties and survive today as the "Pennsylvania Dutch."

Like the Quakers, they believed in nonresistance and absolute pacifism. They differed from the Friends in their belief that the material world was so hopelessly corrupt as to defy redemption. No Christian, they argued, could participate in worldly ways without himself being corrupted by them. Thus, they withdrew into their own tightly-sealed societies and, except for supporting Quakers electorally, did not participate in building the Holy Experiment. They have never really comprised an anti-war "movement" but to the present day have resisted military service as conscientious objectors. Like the Quakers and others who have refused to participate in American wars, they have often suffered cruelly for their beliefs, especially during World War I.

The Jehovah's Witnesses, a relatively young fundamentalist and apocalyptic sect, is pacifistic in the sense that its members refuse to bear arms. But the Witnesses' social conservatism, like Pennsylvania Dutch social withdrawal, has precluded any participation in anti-war movements. Members may serve, for example, in noncombat military capacities and, in October, 1967, some church leaders announced publicly that the sect would have nothing to do with individuals who sought to "use" the Witnesses in order to shirk their "duties" to their country.

Self-styled pacifists have done stranger things. During World War I, a sectarian who was forbidden "to bear arms" consented to military service when he was assigned to the heavy artillery. Another refused to wear a uniform on the grounds that it had buttons which, he patiently explained, were traditionally made of bone retrieved from slaughterhouses.

Other sects whose members refuse to serve in the military have been numerous in American history, but they have exerted no anti-war influence comparable to that of the Quakers. Far more significant have been members of traditionally non-pacifist churches who individually interpreted Christianity as a religion committed against war. These have generally been Protestants and deeply imbued with the "New England conscience": concern for mankind and society as a whole. As a result, they have been no mere conscientious objectors but active agitators for peace.

---

* There are two regions in southwest Germany called Palatinates, once ruled by counts palatine of the Holy Roman Empire.

Early Peace Societies

Such individuals have no doubt always been present in American churches but they emerged as a movement only after the War of 1812. Peace societies were founded independently in Massachusetts, New York, and Ohio during the 1820's and included among their members many prominent ministers of several denominations.

As the historian of the American peace movement, Merle Curti, has explained, the sudden organized interest in peace derived in part from the unpopularity of the War of 1812, especially in New England.* Furthermore, there was a widespread revulsion at the time to the gore and horrors of the Napoleonic wars on the continent of Europe. The New York and Massachusetts societies drew heavily from accounts of the suffering in Europe to drive home their points.

But the origins of the wave of pacifism went deeper, deriving from the idealism of the eighteenth-century Enlightenment, the conviction that man and his society were perfectible. Just as the Quaker commitment to representative government and pacifism derived from their belief that God was within all men, nineteenth-century pacifism derived from the Enlightenment ideal that men were reasonable beings. Protestantism was fundamentally shaken by the Enlightenment and it is not surprising that one of the greatest inheritors of the two traditions, the Unitarian, William Ellery Channing, spoke stridently in the cause of peace.

Not all Unitarians, of course, were pacifists. Nor was pacifism restricted to the sons of the Enlightenment. The scourge of the "corpse cold Unitarianism of Beacon Hill and Brattle Street," Ralph Waldo Emerson (1803–1882), delivered a famous address attacking war, and his sometime friend and fellow Transcendentalist, Henry David Thoreau (1817–1862), went to jail rather than pay taxes which might indirectly support the Mexican War and the expansion of slavery.

With the exception of a few individuals, the Quakers stood aloof from the new peace organizations. In part this was a reflection of the Quaker turn to private piety after the demise of the Holy Experiment. In addition, however, the Friends scorned the policy of some of the new peace societies of allowing for defensive wars as sanctioned by both sacred scripture and the rule of reason. To Quakers and many other pacifists, the distinction between aggressive and defensive war was spurious. Experience proved that any nation could and would claim in wartime that it was defending itself.

Division between absolute pacifists and those who approved defensive war plagued the American Peace Society from its founding in 1828. From a tactical point of view, absolute pacifists argued that preparation for defense invariably led to war and thus rendered any distinction between aggressor and defender impossible. But others retorted that the alternative to condoning defensive war was unequivocal resistance to the government in time of war and that few Americans regarded the United States government as deserving such censure.

---

* See Merle E. Curti, *The American Peace Crusade* (Durham, N. C.: Duke University Press, 1929); and *Peace or War* (Boston: J. S. Conner & Co., 1959).

When the American Peace Society vacillated on this critical question, the "radicals," led by the remarkable "learned blacksmith," Elihu Burritt, formed the New England Resistance Society. No man or body of men had the right to take a life, the Resisters claimed, and no man should collaborate even indirectly with a government which waged war. Members of the Society were enjoined to obey their government except when it bade them disobey their consciences. Then they must resist. Burritt was instrumental in securing 20,000 signatures to such a pledge.

The split in the peace movement did not matter a great deal, for when the crisis came neither faction displayed much devotion to its ideal. The American Peace Society devoted its time to finding justifications for the war instead of opposing it. The Society fell back on the old technicality that it condemned only "international wars" and therefore supported the bloodiest war of the century because it was "civil." But even the fiery resisters, with the exception of a few stalwarts like Burritt, were thrown off balance by the Civil War. Instead of 20,000, the number of C.O.'s during the Civil War was only in the hundreds. Like the Pennsylvania Quakers who sacrificed the pacifism of the Holy Experiment to its ideal of representative democracy, the anti-slavery resisters "yielded allegiance to the war-god when with his battle axe he cleft asunder the fetter of the slave."*

The Civil War presents an example of a dilemma which is central to American pacifism, rooted in the fact that the pacifist is usually committed to a major social change of one sort or another. Pacifism itself is revolutionary; inasmuch as mankind has not even begun to eliminate war after 5,000 years of history, pacifism may be seeking the most fundamental of revolutions.

Unsurprisingly, pacifists have generally been interested in other movements to transform society. The pre–Civil War peace societies are a good example of how these other interests sometimes sapped pacifist efforts of their strength. Some pacifists argued, for example, that peace could be secured on earth only when all men were Christians and they therefore diverted energies and monies to the missionary movement. Other pacifists were distracted by an evil that was more compelling in peacetime, the existence of racial slavery in the United States.

Anti-slavery societies were always better supported than peace societies, and, when abolition was tacitly adopted as a war aim by the Union, notable former pacifists like William Lloyd Garrison and Charles Sumner supported the war with enthusiasm.

At the root of every pacifist's ideal, whatever his rationale, was a compassion for the human suffering caused by war. Yet what to do when human suffering from other causes seemed so great that the resort to arms looked like the only answer? Margaret Fuller expressed the usual pacifist solution in a letter to American pacifist friends from revolution-torn Rome in 1848: "What you say about the Peace Way is deeply true. If anyone can see clearly how to work in that way, let him, in God's name. Only, if he abstain from giant wrongs, let him be sure he is really and ardently at work undermining them, or better still, sus-

---

* Curti, *American Peace Crusade*, p. 87.

taining the rights that are to supplant them. Meanwhile, I am not sure that I can keep my hands free from blood."*

Margaret Fuller's dilemma has come to have even greater meaning for American pacifists of the twentieth century. Social revolution today means some form of socialism; and the socialist impulse has been deeply affected by the Russian example of success through violence. For socialists like Norman Thomas who incline to pacifism and also reject the Bolshevik way, this has presented no logical problem. For pacifists critical yet defensive of the Soviet Union like Reverend A. J. Muste, it has been a troublesome dilemma requiring painstaking deliberation.

The appearance of Fascism in Italy and Germany, glorifying war and hostile as well to the kind of social change which pacifists espoused, exacerbated the problem. Fascism was national criminality, utterly unresponsive to the moral pressures American pacifists were accustomed to employing at home. Moreover, Fascism clearly aimed at a career of conquest which most armies, let alone pacifist nonresistance, seemed unable to stop. Pacifists like the Quakers who regarded their ideal as primarily a matter of personal piety had no trouble in maintaining their course. But, like abolitionist-pacifists during the Civil War, many socialist-pacifists of the 1930's found themselves rallying to the flag when the United States committed itself to the anti-Fascist alliance.

Pacifist Groups in the Twentieth Century

As it always has in post-war periods, the peace movement which emerged from the American Civil War benefited from the nation's recognition of the scope of the slaughter the war had perpetrated. But the circumstances which postwar pacifists confronted were also quite different from what they had previously known. For one thing was the appearance of organizations actually pitted against the pacifist ideal. Veterans' organizations like the Grand Army of the Republic, at first devoted primarily to dividing a treasury surplus among its members in the form of pensions, glorified the Civil War with an abandon that implied the veterans were none too sure of their memories. In fact, the further the war receded into dim memory, the more intense became the romanticization of it. The G.A.R. and newly founded patriotic clubs like the Daughters of the American Revolution developed into forerunners of the contemporary American Legion, anticipating future wars as well as remembering those past, and stifling voices raised against either.

Not until the coming of the American Legion, however, would pacifists find a superior match among the superpatriots. The epoch following the Civil War, despite the aberration of the brief war with Spain, was a time of peace. The first decade of the twentieth century, in fact, as Merle Curti has written, was a time when the peace movement was "universally popular. . . . Even the more cautious and realistic believed that the dawn of peace could not be far off, if it was not already at hand."†

---

* Curti, *Peace or War*, p. 45.
† *Ibid.*, p. 196.

Growing labor unions regularly echoed anti-war sentiments. Burgeoning radical organizations such as the Socialist Party of America denounced at least national wars. The American Peace Society, still the focus of the movement, prospered in membership and revenues.

And the peace movement basked in the prestige of support given by such prominent capitalists as the Boston publisher Edward Ginn, Jacob Schiff, Andrew Carnegie (the most unlikely of all since part of his fortune had been made selling armor plate to the Navy), and later, Henry Ford. The interest of such men was a mixed blessing because their influence turned organizations like the American Peace Society toward social conservatism and deprived the pacifists of the insights into the causes of war offered by radicals. The economic sources of war were little noticed by American pacifists. Instead, their organizations were often saddled with their benefactors' vagaries such as Andrew Carnegie's conviction that Wilhelm II of Germany was the man of destiny who would usher in Europe's pacifist millenium.

But, in the short run, the movement's conservatism seemed to mean only quadrupled budgets and membership and names on the roster like William Jennings Bryan and Woodrow Wilson.

Pacifist optimism was rudely shocked by the outbreak of war in Europe in 1914 and the halting path of the United States toward entrance into the conflict. Hurried attempts to influence events were uniformly futile. Pacifists, especially through their highly placed ally, Secretary of State Bryan, urged President Wilson to offer his services as a mediator. But the President was distracted by the failing health of his wife and befuddled by the European explosion. In December, 1915, Henry Ford led an expedition of luminaries on the chartered ship, *Oscar II*, to Europe. But the voyage was self-parodied by the expedition's own hoopla, mercilessly lampooned in the press, torn by dissensions aboard ship (Ford himself abandoned the project in Oslo, Norway), and not precisely calculated to influence a continent in flames in the first place.

Pacifist attempts to keep the United States out of the war seemed more kindly fated. American sentiment, until the very eve of the nation's declaration, seemed overwhelmingly opposed to involvement. "I Didn't Raise My Boy to Be a Soldier" was a popular song and President Wilson ran for re-election in 1916 partly on the slogan, "He Kept Us Out of War." But warhawks like Theodore Roosevelt had become numerous. Effective British propaganda in the United States, German blunders, Wilson's increasingly pro-allied sentiments, the depredations of German submarines, and the clamor of American investors in the allied war effort combined to push the United States into the conflict.

The patriotic hysteria of World War I and its aftermath is unparalleled in American history and many members of the various peace societies, as usual, jumped enthusiastically on the caissons. Many others remained firm in their convictions and suffered severely from both informal and governmental repression. Treatment of conscientious objectors was notoriously poor. Fred A. Robinson, arrested in Washington state for failing to comply with the draft law, issued a statement upon his arrest in which he said, "I, as an ambassador of Christ, have decided to be loyal to my King. Having considered this question carefully from God's viewpoint . . . and considered the penalties, I cannot conscientiously obey this order of induction into military service." Robinson could not have anticipated the penalty he was awarded; he was classified as a deserter and sentenced to be shot. This was later commuted to twenty-five years imprisonment. At Camp Grant in Illinois, an objector was fed only bread and water, handcuffed so that he had to stand all day, and handcuffed to his bed at night. Nor was this torture unusual. At Camp Upton, a C.O. was stuck and cut repeatedly on his knees and shins with bayonets. At one point he was beaten steadily for two hours with fists and rifle butts. Several conscientious objectors died in prison under suspicious circumstances.*

On the whole, however, the great opposition to World War I was not a pacifist but a radical movement. If this had no other effect on the pacifists, it taught them to pay more attention to the long-neglected economic causes of war and diverted them from their prewar conservatism to a closer relationship with radical groups. The American Civil Liberties Union, founded in reaction to the wartime mockery of civil liberties, defended both religious and radical pacifists. New organizations replaced the American Peace Society, which ceased to exist during the twenties. The Fellowship of Reconciliation, the War Resisters International, and the Women's International League for Peace and Freedom maintained close relations with radical organizations and incorporated radical thought into their programs.

By the thirties the economic origins of war were no longer neglected. In his second book on the history of the peace movement, Merle Curti pointed it out as a major weakness of the peace movement that "peacemakers have not adequately fought the economic forces that make for war."† But this was no longer true by the date of Curti's work, 1936, which, as a pro-pacifist tract as well as a work of scholarship, proves the point by its own emphasis.

The new emphasis on social change also contributed to the partial collapse of pacifism during World War II. Social radicals, including many pacifists, viewed Naziism as a threat to social progress which would respond only to force. But other pacifists, in great numbers, kept the faith. Over 5,000 conscientious objectors, chiefly pacifists, were imprisoned during the war, eight times as many as during World War I. Their treatment was considerably improved, although the average sentence for a C.O. (30.6 months) seemed out of all proportion to sentences meted out during the same period to narcotics offenders (20.8 months), liquor law offenders (20.8 months), postal law offenders (27.3 months), and white slave law offenders (28.3 months).

Since World War II, pacifism has remained a visible if not determinant influence in American affairs. While the Cold War has served to stimulate superpatriotism and militarism, the spectre of nuclear war has provided pacifist organizations with a new reason why they should be heard. The horror of nuclear war

---

* H. C. Peterson and Gilbert C. Fite, *Opponents of War* (Madison University of Wisconsin Press, 1957), p. 132.

† Curti, *Peace or War*, p. 176.

has given peace societies like the Fellowship of Reconciliation their chief talking point. Joined by an increasingly active Society of Friends, pacifists have performed dramatic acts of defiance—for instance, sailing boats into areas in which the United States was exploding nuclear devices.

By the late fifties, pacifist groups had almost uniformly turned to the direct confrontation and defiance once preached only by Elihu Burritt's off-shoot of the American Peace Society. Quakers, other Protestant pacifists, and members of the Catholic Worker organization have defied air-raid drills in New York and other cities with the challenge that "Peace is our only shelter," and numerous groups have suggested that their members refuse to pay at least that part of their taxes expended on the military.

Another basic thrust of the recent peace movement has been internationalism. The idea of an association of nations as an alternative to war for the settlement of international differences has been espoused in America as far back as William Penn. Pacifists of the early twentieth century enthusiastically supported arbitration treaties such as those devised by William Jennings Bryan as Secretary of State. The peace movement of the twenties lamented the failure of the United States to join the League of Nations and supported the American movement to ratify the Kellogg–Briand Pact, which "outlawed" war as an instrument of national policy.

Most pacifists since 1945 have been enthusiastic supporters of the United Nations as an invaluable, if disappointing, hope for world peace. Some pacifist organizations such as the United World Federalists have devoted themselves primarily to the strenghtening of international peacekeeping machinery and propagandizing for world government.

While American pacifism has been primarily a Protestant phenomenon, the Catholic Worker Movement has, since its founding in 1933, been a prominent exception. The Movement was the joint undertaking of Peter Maurin and Dorothy Day, both pious Catholics who were also radicals. While their pacifism drew from the same Christian traditions to which Quakers and Protestant pacifists looked, it has a decided Catholic flavor, at least in its reliance on the writings of strictly Catholic saints.

Saint John of the Cross' aphorism, "Where there is no love, put in love and you will take out love" stands at the center of Catholic Worker thought. Like the Quakers, the workers in the movement devote their lives to charity, operating Hospitality Houses (where homeless men may take a meal and a bed) in several cities and cooperative farms organized and operated on anarchist principles.

The movement is also absolutely pacifistic. Its members refuse to serve in the armed forces and even to collaborate with the Selective Service and pay no taxes which are used for military purposes. (This is usually no problem, for Catholic Workers live in voluntary poverty and rarely make enough to be eligible for taxation.)

Because of its social radicalism, the Catholic Worker Movement has never consisted of more than a few hundred active workers. Less extreme organizations

such as the Catholic Peace Fellowship, however, have served to voice the views
of many more Roman Catholic pacifists.

A Declaration against All Plotters and Fighters (1660)

George Fox and other Quakers

The Quakers suffered mightily in Stuart England for their beliefs. (At one
time very nearly every adult Quaker in the realm was in prison.) On the occasion
of one widespread harassment, George Fox and eleven other Friends addressed
the King with a succinct explanation of Quaker pacifism and a plea to spare the
Society the King's wrath.

The letter, dated November 21, 1660 in *The Journal of George Fox*, is valuable
as a compilation of those biblical admonitions on which not only the Quakers,
but many other Christians, based their pacifism. The letter is also of interest
because it illustrates a conservative streak in Quakerism which, at other times,
would be de-emphasized, namely the Friends' obeisant acceptance of legitimate
authority except when it collided directly with their consciences. Fox and the
others relied on the King's recognition of this conservatism to lead him to lift
the persecution and, for the time at least, he did. "There was a great darkness
both in the city and country," Fox wrote, "but this declaration of ours cleared the
air and laid the darkness, and the King gave forth after this a little proclamation
that no soldiers should go to search any house but with a constable [and] the
King gave forth after this a declaration that Friends should be set at liberty
without paying fees." Fox is almost exultant in his *Journal*, in fact, that genuine
conspirators against the crown were soundly punished. Twenty years later,
Quakers were sufficiently accepted by the British crown that William Penn was
granted a colony in North America.

*A Declaration from the harmless and innocent people of God, called
Quakers, against all plotters and fighters in the world,* for the removing
the ground of jealousy and suspicion from both magistrates and people
in the kingdom, concerning wars and fightings. And also something in
answer to that clause of the King's late Proclamation which mentions
the Quakers, to clear them from the plot and fighting which therein
is mentioned, and for the clearing their innocency.

Our principle is, and our practices have always been to seek peace
and ensue it and to follow after righteousness and the knowledge of
God, seeking the good and welfare and doing that which tends to the
peace of all. We know that wars and fightings proceed from the lusts

of men (as Jas. 4:1–3), out of which lusts the Lord hath redeemed us, and so out of the occasion of war. The occasion of which war, and war itself (wherein envious men, who are lovers of themselves more than lovers of God, lust, kill, and desire to have men's lives or estates) ariseth from the lust. All bloody principles and practices, we, as to our own particulars, do utterly deny, with all outward wars and strife and fightings with outward weapons, for any end or under any pretence whatsoever. And this is our testimony to the whole world.

And whereas it is objected:

"But although you now say that you cannot fight nor take up arms at all, yet if the spirit do move you, then you will change your principle, and then you will sell your coat and buy a sword and fight for the kingdom of Christ."

Answer:

As for this we say to you that Christ said to Peter, "Put up thy sword in his place"; though he had said before, he that had no sword might sell his coat and buy one (to the fulfilling of the law and Scripture), yet after, when he had bid him put it up, he said, "He that taketh the sword shall perish with the sword." And further, Christ said to Peter, "Thinkest thou, that I cannot now pray to my Father, and he shall presently give me more than twelve legions of angels?" And this might satisfy Peter, after he had put up his sword, when he said to him he that took it, should perish by it, which satisfieth us. (Luke 12:36; Matt. 16:51–53.) And in the Revelation, it's said, "He that kills with the sword shall perish with the sword: and here is the faith and the patience of the saints." (Rev. 13:10.) And so Christ's kingdom is not of this world, therefore do not his servants fight, as he told Pilate, the magistrate who crucified him. And did they not look upon Christ as a raiser of sedition? And did not he say, "Forgive them"? But thus it is that we are numbered amongst transgressors and numbered amongst fighters, that the Scriptures might be fulfilled.

That the spirit of Christ, by which we are guided, is not changeable, so as once to command us from a thing as evil and again to move unto it; and we do certainly know, and so testify to the world, that the spirit of Christ, which leads us into all truth, will never move us to fight and war against any man with outward weapons, neither for the kingdom of Christ, nor for the kingdoms of this world.

First:

Because the kingdom of Christ God will exalt, according to his promise, and cause it to grow and flourish in righteousness. "Not by might, nor by power [of outward sword], but by my spirit, saith the Lord." (Zech. 4:6.) So those that use any weapon to fight for Christ, or for the establishing of his kingdom or government, both the spirit, principle, and practice in that we deny.

Secondly:

And as for the kingdoms of this world, we cannot covet them, much less can we fight for them, but we do earnestly desire and wait, that by the word of God's power and its effectual operation in the hearts of men, the kingdoms of this world may become the kingdoms of the Lord, and of his Christ, that he may rule and reign in men by his spirit and truth, that thereby all people, out of all different judgements and professions may be brought into love and unity with God, and one with another, and that they may all come to witness the prophet's words who said, "Nation shall not lift up sword against nation, neither shall they learn war any more." (Isa. 2:4; Mic. 4:3.)

So, we whom the Lord hath called into the obedience of his truth have denied wars and fightings and cannot again any more learn it. This is a certain testimony unto all the world of the truth of our hearts in this particular, that as God persuadeth every man's heart to believe, so they may receive it. For we have not, as some others, gone about cunningly with devised fables, nor have we ever denied in practice what we have professed in principle, but in sincerity and truth and by the word of God have we labored to be made manifest unto all men, that both we and our ways might be witnessed in the hearts of all people.

And whereas all manner of evil hath been falsely spoken of us, we hereby speak forth the plain truth of our hearts, to take away the occasion of that offence, that so we being innocent may not suffer for other men's offences, nor be made a prey upon by the wills of men for that of which we were never guilty; but in the uprightness of our hearts we may, under the power ordained of God for the punishment of evil-doers and for the praise of them that do well, live a peaceable and godly life in all godliness and honesty. For although we have always suffered, and do now more abundantly suffer, yet we know that it's for righteousness' sake; "for all our rejoicing is this, the testimony of our consciences, that in simplicity and godly sincerity, not with fleshly wisdom but by the grace of God, we have had our conversation in the world" (II Cor. 1:12), which for us is a witness for the convincing of our enemies. For this we can say to the whole world, we have wronged no man's person or possessions, we have used no force nor violence against any man, we have been found in no plots, nor guilty of sedition. When we have been wronged, we have not sought to revenge ourselves, we have not made resistance against authority, but wherein we could not obey for conscience' sake, we have suffered even the most of any people in the nation. We have been accounted as sheep for the slaughter, persecuted and despised, beaten, stoned, wounded, stocked, whipped, imprisoned, haled out of synagogues, cast into dungeons and noisome vaults where many have died in bonds, shut up from our friends, denied needful sustenance for many days together, with other the like cruelties.

And the cause of all this our sufferings is not for any evil, but for things relating to the worship of our God and in obedience to his requirings of us. For which cause we shall freely give up our bodies a sacrifice, rather than disobey the Lord. For we know, as the Lord hath kept us innocent, so he will plead our cause, when there is none in the earth to plead it. So we, in obedience unto his truth, do not love our lives unto the death, that we may do his will, and wrong no man in our generation, but seek the good and peace of all men. And he that hath commanded us that we shall not swear at all (Matt. 5:34), hath also commanded us that we shall not kill (Matt. 5:21), so that we can neither kill men, nor swear for not against them. And this is both our principle and practice, and hath been from the beginning, so that if we suffer, as suspected to take up arms or make war against any, it is without any ground from us; for it neither is, nor ever was in our hearts, since we owned the truth of God; neither shall we ever do it, because it is contrary to the spirit of Christ, his doctrine, and the practice of his apostles, even contrary to him for whom we suffer all things, and endure all things.

And whereas men come against us with clubs, staves, drawn swords, pistols cocked, and do beat, cut, and abuse us, yet we never resisted them, but to them our hair, backs, and cheeks have been ready. It is not an honour to manhood nor to nobility to run upon harmless people who lift not up a hand against them, with arms and weapons.

Therefore consider these things ye men of understanding; for plotters, raisers of insurrections, tumultuous ones, and fighters, running with swords, clubs, staves, and pistols one against another, we say, these are of the world and this hath its foundation from this unrighteous world, from the foundation of which the Lamb hath been slain, which Lamb hath redeemed us from the unrighteous world, and we are not of it, but are heirs of a world in which there is no end and of a kingdom where no corruptible thing enters. And our weapons are spiritual and not carnal, yet mighty through God to the plucking down of the strongholds of Satan, who is author of wars, fighting, murder, and plots. And our swords are broken into ploughshares and spears into pruning-hooks, as prophesied of in Micah, chapter four. Therefore we cannot learn war any more, neither rise up against nation or kingdom with outward weapons, though you have numbered us among the transgressors and plotters. The Lord knows our innocency herein, and will plead our cause with all men and people upon earth at the day of their judgement, when all men shall have a reward according to their works. . . .

O friends offend not the Lord and his little ones, neither afflict his people, but consider and be moderate, and do not run hastily into things, but mind and consider mercy, justice, and judgement; that is the way for you to prosper and get the favour of the Lord. Our meetings were stopped and broken up in the days of Oliver [Cromwell], in pretence of plotting against him; and in the days of the Parliament and Committee of Safety we were looked upon as plotters to bring in King Charles, and now we are called plotters against King Charles. Oh, that men should lose their reason and go contrary to their own conscience, knowing that we have suffered all things and have been accounted plotters all along, though we have declared against them both by word of mouth and printing, and are clear from any such things. We have suffered all along because we would not take up carnal weapons to fight withal against any, and are thus made a prey upon because we are the innocent lambs of Christ and cannot avenge ourselves. These things are left upon your hearts to consider, but we are out of all those things in the patience of the saints, and we know that as Christ said, "He that takes the sword, shall perish with the sword." (Matt. 26:52; Rev. 13:10.)

This is given forth from the people called Quakers to satisfy the King and his Council, and all those that have any jealousy concerning us, that all occasion of suspicion may be taken away and our innocency cleared.

Given forth under our names, and in behalf of the whole body of the Elect People of God who are called Quakers.

GEORGE FOX	GERRARD ROBERTS	HENRY FELL
RICHARD HUBBERTHORN	JOHN BOLTON	JOHN HINDE
JOHN STUBBS	LEONARD FELL	JOHN FURLEY JUNR.
FRANCIS HOWGILL	SAMUEL FISHER	THOMAS MOORE

Postscript.—Though we are numbered with plotters in this late Proclamation and put in the midst of them and numbered amongst transgressors and so have been given up to all rude, merciless men, by which our meetings are broken up, in which we edified one another in our holy faith and prayed together to the Lord that lives for ever, yet he is our pleader for us in this day. The Lord saith, "They that feared his name spoke often together," as in Malachi, which were as his jewels. And for this cause and no evil doing, are we cast into holes, dungeons, houses of correction, prisons, they sparing neither old nor young, men or women, and just sold to all nations and made a prey to all nations under pretence of being plotters, so that all rude people run upon us to take possession. For which we say, "The Lord forgive them that have thus done to us," who doth and will enable us to suffer. And never shall we lift up a hand against any man that doth thus use us, but that the Lord may have mercy upon them, that they may consider what they have done. For how is it hardly possible for them to requite us for the wrong they have done to us, who to all nations have sounded us abroad as plotters? We who were never found plotters against any power or man upon the earth since we knew the life and power of Jesus Christ manifested in us, who hath redeemed us from the world, and all works of darkness, and plotters that be in it, by which we know our election before the world began. So we say the Lord have mercy upon our enemies and forgive them, for that they have done unto us.

Oh, do as you would be done by. And do unto all men as you would have them do unto you, for this is but the law and the prophets.

And all plots, insurrections, and riotous meetings we do deny, knowing them to be of the devil, the murderer, which we in Christ, which was before they were, triumph over. And all wars and fightings with carnal weapons we do deny, who have the sword of the spirit; and all that wrong us we leave to the Lord. And this is to clear our innocency from that aspersion cast upon us, that we are plotters. . . .

Towards Present and Future Peace (1693)*

William Penn

Although the Quakers emphasized the fact that they did not threaten the status quo, neither Penn nor the other Quakers were trucklers after the public favor. In the Quaker manner, which distinguishes the Society from purely personal pacifists, Penn was interested in and agitated for the rule of peace throughout the world (which to him, of course, was Europe and its territories). In the book from which this piece is excerpted, first published in 1693, Penn outlined a plan

---

* From William Penn, *An Essay towards the Present and Future Peace of Europe, by the Establishment of an European Diet, Parliament, or Estates.* Reprinted in *International Conciliation* (November, 1943).

for an international organization which, through just settlements of international disputes, would ordain such a realm. His plea was addressed to non-Quakers, so he wasted little time in arguing the spiritual nature of peace. Rather, as this first section of the essay illustrates, Penn was willing to argue for peace on any honest grounds, a characteristic which has remained typical of the society. (The supremely modest tone of the introduction is no special reflection of Penn's personality; it was a convention of that time.)

To the Reader:

I have undertaken a subject that, I am very sensible, requires one of more sufficiency than I am master of to treat it as in truth it deserves and the groaning state of Europe calls for; but since bunglers may stumble upon the game as well as masters, though it belongs to the skillful to hunt and catch it, I hope this essay will not be charged upon me for a fault, if it appear to be neither chimerical nor injurious, and may provoke abler pens to improve and perform the design with better judgment and success. I will say no more in excuse of myself for this undertaking but that it is the fruit of many solicitous thoughts for the peace of Europe, and they must want charity as much as the world needs quiet to be offended with me for so pacific a proposal. Let them censure my management, so they prosecute the advantage of the design; for till the millenary doctrine be accomplished,* there is nothing appears to be so beneficial an expedient to the peace and happiness of this quarter of the world.

Of Peace and Its Advantages

He must not be a man but a statue of brass or stone, whose bowels do not melt when he beholds the bloody tragedies of this war in Hungary, Flanders, Ireland, and at sea; the mortality of sickly and languishing camps and navies; and the mighty prey the devouring winds and waves have made upon ships and men since 1688. And as this with reason ought to affect human nature, and deeply kindred, so there is something very moving that becomes prudent men to consider, and that is the vast charge that has accompanied that blood, and which makes no mean part of these tragedies; especially if they deliberate upon the uncertainty of the war, that they know not when nor how it will end, and that the expense cannot be less and the hazard is as great as before. So that in the contraries of peace we see the beauties and benefits of it, which under it—such is the unhappiness of mankind—

---

* Penn was referring to the common Christian belief in the *millennium*, or thousand-year Kingdom of God on earth, which was expected by many to arrive soon with the Second Coming of Christ. For a modern version of this doctrine, see the selection on the Jehovah's Witnesses later in this chapter.

we are too apt to nauseate, as the full stomach loathes the honeycomb, and like that unfortunate gentleman that, having a fine and a good woman to his wife and searching his pleasure in forbidden and less agreeable company, said, when reproached with his neglect of better enjoyments, that he could love his wife of all women if she were not his wife, though that increased his obligation to prefer her. It is a great mark of the corruption of our natures, and what ought to humble us extremely and excite the exercise of our reason to a nobler and juster sense, that we cannot see the use and pleasure of our comforts but by the want of them. As if we could not taste the benefit of health but by the help of sickness, nor understand the satisfaction of fullness without the instruction of want, nor, finally, know the comfort of peace but by the smart and penance of the vices of war—and without dispute that is not the least reason that God is pleased to chastise us so frequently with it.

What can we desire better than peace but the grace to use it? Peace preserves our possessions: we are in no danger of invasions, our trade is free and safe, and we rise and lie down without anxiety. The rich bring out their hoards and employ the poor manufactors. Buildings and divers projections for profit and pleasure go on. It excites industry, which brings wealth, as that gives the means of charity and hospitality, not the lowest ornaments of a kingdom or commonwealth. But war, like the frost of '83, seizes all these comforts at once, and stops the civil channel of society. The rich draw in their stock, the poor turn soldiers or thieves, or starve: no industry, no building, no manufactury, little hospitality or charity; but what the peace gave the war devours. I need say no more upon this head, when the advantages of peace and mischiefs of war are so many and sensible in every capacity under all governments, as either of them prevails.

War and Wealth (1763)

John Woolman

Lacking the prominence of Fox and Penn, John Woolman was a pious New Jersey Quaker who spent most of his life in selfless wanderings on behalf of the Friendly Persuasion. He authored a *Journal* and a variety of essays. The former is considered a minor masterpiece of English prose, reflecting the simplicity and precision which were peculiarly Quaker virtues.

Woolman was familiar with the evils of his world, if decidedly not a part of them. Like Quakers before and since, he concentrated his attentions on the most blatant ones. Thus, although he commented at some length on the frequent Indian wars of his lifetime, Woolman—an Easterner, not a frontiersman—was more occupied with matters such as slavery and avarice in trade.

But he did comment on war, gently, of course. This excerpt, Chapter Ten of *A Plea for the Poor*, written in 1763, is interesting chiefly for Woolman's insights into the economic origins of war, a vision usually attributed to another age and certainly an altogether different kind of person. The book was published in London, 1793.

"Are not two sparrows sold for a farthing, and one of them shall not fall to the ground without your father."

The way of carrying on wars, common in the world, is so far distinguishable from the purity of Christ's religion, that many scruple to join in them. Those who are so redeemed from the love of the world, as to possess nothing in a selfish spirit, their "life is hid with Christ in God," and these he preserves in resignedness, even in times of commotion.

As they possess nothing but what pertains to his family, anxious thoughts about wealth or dominion hath little or nothing in them to work upon, and they learn contentment in being disposed or according to his will, who being omnipotent, and always mindful of his children, causeth all things to work for their good. But where that spirit works which loves riches; works, and in its working gathers wealth, and cleaves to customs which have their root in self pleasing. This spirit thus separating from universal love, seeks help from that power which stands in the separation, and whatever name it hath, it still desireth to defend the treasures thus gotten. This is like a chain, where the end of one link encloses the end of another. The rising up of a desire to obtain wealth is the beginning. This desire being cherished moves to action, and riches thus gotten please self and while self hath a life in them it desires to have them defended.

Wealth is attended with power, by which bargains and proceedings contrary to universal righteousness are supported, and here oppression, carried on with worldly policy and order, clothes itself with the name of justice, and becomes like a seed of discord in the soil: and as this spirit which wanders from the pure habitation prevails, so the seed of war swells and sprouts and grows and becomes strong, till much fruit are ripened. Thus cometh the harvest spoken of by the prophet, which "is a heap, in the day of grief and of desperate sorrow."

Oh! that we who declare against wars, and acknowledge our trust to be in God only, may walk in the light, and therein examine our foundation and motives in holding great estates: may we look upon our treasures, and the furniture of our houses, and the garments in which we array ourselves, and try whether the seeds of war have any nourishment in these our possessions, or not. Holding treasures in the self pleasing spirit is a strong plant, the fruit whereof ripens fast.

A day of outward distress is coming, and divine love calls to prepare for it. Hearken then, O ye children who have known the light, and come forth! Leave every thing which our Lord Jesus Christ does not own. Think not his pattern too plain or too coarse for you. Think not a small portion in this life too little: but let us live in his spirit, and walk as he walked, and he will preserve us in the greatest troubles.

The True Grandeur of Nations (1845)*

Charles Sumner

Charles Sumner (1811–1874), one of the pivotal figures of mid–nineteenth-century American politics, delivered one of his most notable speeches, "The True Grandeur of Nations," in Boston on Independence Day, 1845—the eve of the Mexican War. It is difficult to fathom the personal courage (and sense of irony) which Sumner's speech represented. The Fourth of July is a day for bombastic patriotic rhetoric when—and 1845 was no exception—flags fly, uni-formed soldiers march about, and Americans come closest to glorifying war itself. Boston was in 1845, moreover, more than usually martial as the nation moved toward war with Mexico. In such an atmosphere, Sumner attacked war.

Sumner was a lifelong exponent of reformist causes, only one of which was pacifism. A leading abolitionist, Sumner was only one of many pacifists who, faced with the cruel choice of opposing the Civil War in 1861 or supporting it as a means of shattering the institution of slavery, chose the latter. But in 1845 Sumner could in conscience support both pacifist and abolitionist causes with all his New England ardor and oratorical genius. In fact, Sumner and many abolitionists damned the Mexican War because, in addition to their pacifism, they saw the conflict as a land grab by Southern slavocrats.

This short excerpt from Sumner's speech cannot begin to provide the savor of either Sumner's grandiose rhetoric or the involvement of his argument. Ora-tions were incredibly long by the standards of our hurried world (one text of

* Excerpted from *The Works of Charles Sumner* (Boston: Lee & Shepard, 1870–83), I, 1–132.

"The True Grandeur of Nations" runs 133 pages) and Bostonians liked theirs
laced with quotations from the classics, scripture, and more recent literature.

If nothing else, Sumner was comprehensive. Traces appear in the speech
of the traditional Christian anti-war spirit, humanistic revulsion at the excesses
of war, hardheaded Yankee chagrin at the dollars-and-cents wastefulness of
war, and topical slaps at the federal government's bellicosity. It is one of the
classics of American anti-war literature.

It well becomes the patriot citizen, on this anniversary, to consider
the national character, and how it may be advanced—as the good man
dedicates his birthday to meditation on his life, and to resolutions of
improvement. Avoiding, then, all exultation in the abounding prosperity of the land, and in that freedom whose influence is widening to
the uttermost circles of the earth, I would turn attention to the character of our country, and humbly endeavor to learn what must be done
that the republic may best secure the welfare of the people committed
to its care—that it may perform its part in the world's history—that
it may fulfill the aspirations of generous hearts—and, practising that
righteousness which exalteth a nation, attain to the elevation of true
grandeur.

With this aim, and believing that I can in no other way so fitly
fulfil the trust reposed in me today, I purpose to consider what, in our
age, are the true objects of national ambition—*what is truly national
honor, national glory*—WHAT IS THE TRUE GRANDEUR OF NATIONS.
I would not depart from the modesty that becomes me, yet I am not
without hope that I may do something to rescue these terms, now so
powerful over the minds of men, from mistaken objects, especially
from deeds of war, and the extension of empire, that they may be
applied to works of justice and beneficence, which are better than
war or empire.

.   .   .   .

Can there be in our age any peace that is not honorable, any war
that is not dishonorable? The true honor of a nation is conspicuous
only in deeds of justice and beneficence, securing and advancing human
happiness. In the clear eye of that Christian judgement which must
yet prevail, vain are the victories of war, infamous spoils. He is the
benefactor, and worthy of honor, who carries comfort to wretchedness,
cries the tear of sorrow, relieves the unfortunate, feeds the hungry,
clothes the naked, does justice, enlightens the ignorant, unfastens the
fetters of the slave, and finally, by virtuous genius, in art, literature,
science, enlivens and exalts the hours of life, or, by generous example,
inspires a love for God in man. This is the Christian here; this is the

man of honor in a Christian land. He is no benefactor, nor worthy of honor, whatever his worldly renown, whose life is absorbed in feats of brute force, who renounces the great law of Christian brotherhood, whose vocation is blood.

. . . [But] the voice of man is yet given to martial praise, and the hours of victory are chanted even by the lips of woman. The mother, rocking the infant on her knee, stamps the images of war upon his tender mind, at that age more impressible than wax; she nurses his slumber with its music, pleases his waking hours with its stories, and selects for his playthings the plume and the sword. From the child is formed the man; and who can weigh the influence of a mother's spirit on the opinions of his life? . . . And when the youth becomes a man, his country invites his service in war, and holds before his bewildered imagination the prizes of worldly honor. . . . His soul is taught to swell at the thought that he, too, is a soldier—that his name shall be entered on the list of those who have borne arms for their country; and perhaps he dreams that he, too, may sleep, like the great captain of Spain, with a hundred trophies over his grave. The law of the land throws its sanction over this frenzy. The contagion spread beyond those subject to positive obligation. Peaceful citizens volunteer to appear as soldiers, and affect, in dress, arms, and deportment, what is called the "pride, pomp, and circumstance of glorious war." The ear-piercing fife has today filled our streets, and we have come to this church, on this national sabbath, by the thump of drum and with the parade of bristling bayonets.

I would now define the evil which I arraign. *War is a public armed contest between nations, under the sanction of international law, to establish* JUSTICE *between them:* as, for instance, to determine a disputed boundary, the title to territory, or a claim for damages. . . .

It forms no part of my purpose to consider individual wars in the past, except so far as necessary by way of example. My aim is higher. I wish to expose an irrational, cruel, and impious *custom,* sanctioned by the Law of Nations.

After considering, in succession, *first* the character of war, *secondly* the miseries it produces, and, *thirdly* its utter and pitiful insufficiency as a mode of determining justice, we shall be able to decide, strictly and logically, whether it must not be ranked as crime from which no true honor can spring to individuals or nations. . . .

I

First, as to the essential character and root of war, or that part
of our nature whence it proceeds.

.   .   .   .

From early fields of modern literature, as from those of antiquity,
might be gathered . . . illustrations, showing the unconscious degrada-
tion of the soldier, in vain pursuit of *justice*, renouncing his human
character to assume that of brute. Bayard, the exemplar of chivalry,
with a name always on the lips of its votaries, was described by the
qualities of beasts, being, according to his admirers, *ram in attack,
wild boar in defence, and wolf in flight*. Henry V, as represented by our
own Shakespeare, in the spirit-stirring appeal to his troops exclaims,

> When the blast of war blows in our ears,
> Then imitate the action of the tiger.

This is plain and frank, revealing the true character of war.

I need not dwell on the moral debasement that must ensue. Passions,
like so many bloodhounds, are unleashed and suffered to rage. Crimes
filling our prisons stalk abroad in the soldier's garb, unwhipped of
justice. Murder, robbery, rape, arson, are the sports of this fiendish
Saturnalia, when

> The gates of mercy shall be all shut up,
> And the fleshed soldier, rough and hard of heart,
> In liberty of bloodly hand shall range
> With conscience wide as hell.

By a bold, but truthful touch, Shakespeare thus pictures the foul
disfigurement which war produces in man, whose native capacities he
describes in those beautiful words: "How noble in reason! How infinite
in faculties! in form and moving how express and admirable! in action
how like an angel! in apprehension how like a god!" And yet this
nobility of reason, this infinitude of faculties, this marvel of form and
motion, this nature so angelic, so godlike, are all, under the trans-
forming power of war, lost in the action of the beast, or the license of
the fleshed soldier with bloody hand and conscience wide as hell.

II

The immediate effect of war is to sever all relations of friendship
and commerce between the belligerent nations, and every individual
thereof, impressing upon each citizen or subject the character of
enemy. Imagine this instant change between England and the United
States. The innumerable ships of the two countries, the white doves

of commerce, bearing the olive of peace, are driven from the sea, or turned from peaceful purposes to be ministers of destruction; the threads of social and business intercourse, so carefully woven into a thick web, are suddenly snapped asunder; friend can no longer communicate with friend; the twenty thousand letters speeded each fortnight from this port alone are arrested, and the human affections, of which they are the precious expression, seek in vain for utterance. Tell me, you with friends and kindred abroad, or you bound to other lands only by relations of commerce, are you ready for this rude separation?

This is little compared with what must follow. It is but the first portentous shadow of disastrous eclipse, twilight usher of thick darkness, covering the whole heavens with a pall, broken only by the lightnings of battle and siege.

Such horrors redden the historic page, while, to the scandal of humanity, they never want historians with feelings kindred to those by which they are inspired. The demon that draws the sword also guides the pen.

.   .   .   .

My present purpose is less to judge the historian than to expose the horrors on horrors which he applauds. At Tarragona, above six thousand human beings, almost all defenceless men and women, gray hairs and infant innocence, attractive youth and wrinkled age, were butchered by the infuriate troops in one night, and the morning sun rose upon a city whose streets and houses were inundated with blood: and yet this is called a "glorious exploit." Here was a conquest by the French. At a later day, Ciudad Rodrigo was stormed by the British, when, in license of victory, there ensued a savage scene of plunder and violence while shouts and screams on all sides mingled fearfully with the groans of the wounded. Churches were desecrated, cellars of wine and spirits were pillaged, fire was wantonly applied to the city, and brutal intoxication spread in every direction. Only when the drunken dropped from excess or fell asleep, was any degree of order restored: and yet the storming of Ciudad Rodrigo is pronounced "one of the most brilliant exploits of the British army."

.   .   .   .

III

But all these miseries are to no purpose. War is utterly ineffectual to secure or advance its professed object. The wretchedness it entails contributes to no end, helps to establish no right, and therefore in no respect determines *justice* between the contending nations.

The fruitlessness and vanity of war appear in the great conflicts by which the world has been lacerated. After long struggle, where each nation inflicts and receives incalculable injury, peace is gladly obtained on the basis of the condition before the war, known as the *status ante bellum*. I cannot illustrate this futility better than by the familiar example—humiliating to both countries—of our last war with Great Britain, where the professed object was to obtain a renunciation of the British claim, so defiantly asserted, to impress our seamen. To overturn this injustice the arbitrament of war was invoked, and for nearly three years the whole country was under its terrible ban. American commerce was driven from the seas; the resources of the land were drained by taxation; villages on the Canadian frontier were laid in ashes; the metropolis of the republic [Washington, D.C.] was captured; while distress was everywhere within our borders. Weary at last with this rude trial, the national government appointed commissioners to treat for peace, with these specific instructions: "Your first duty will be to conclude a peace with Great Britain; and you are authorized to do it, *in case* you obtain a satisfactory stipulation against impressment, one which shall secure under our flag protection to the crew. . . . If this encroachment of Great Britain is not provided against, *the United States have appealed to arms in vain.*" Afterwards, finding small chance of extorting from Great Britain a relinquishment of the unrighteous claim, and foreseeing from the inveterate prosecution of the war only an accumulation of calamities, the national government directed the negotiators, in concluding a treaty, to "*omit any stipulation on the subject of impressment.*" These instructions were obeyed, and the treaty that restored to us once more the blessings of peace, so rashly cast away, but now hailed with intoxication of joy, contained no allusion to impressment, nor did it provide for the surrender of a single American sailor detained in the British navy. Thus, by the confession of our government, the United States had "*appealed to arms in vain.*" These important words are not mine; they are the words of the country.

Pacifism and Class War (1929)*

A. J. Muste

The problem of reconciling social radicalism with pacifism has been a thorny one on which, most notably, abolitionist-pacifists foundered in 1861 and socialist-democrat-pacifists in 1939. A. J. Muste (1885–1967) remained throughout his long life both a revolutionary and a believer in Christian pacifism. This essay, published in 1929, represents Muste's attempt to come to grips with the dilemma.

Born in the Netherlands, Muste was an ordained minister (Dutch Reformed Church) who opposed World War I, agitated widely on behalf of the organized labor movement, and—in short—took the side of the oppressed in every conflict which came to his attention. An activist to the end, he was a leading organizer of the movement to end the war in Vietnam, actually travelled to Hanoi in an effort to discover National Liberation Front and North Vietnamese terms for peace and died suddenly while planning a rally against the war. Whether or not Muste solved the dilemma of the pacifist revolutionary to universal satisfaction, he never wavered in his own devotion to both causes.

Practically all our thinking about pacifism in connection with class war starts at the wrong point. The question raised is how the oppressed in struggling for freedom and the good life may be dissuaded from employing "the revolutionary method of violence" and won over to "the peaceful process of evolution." Two erroneous assumptions are concealed in the question put that way. The first is that the oppressed, the radicals, are the ones who are creating the disturbance. To the leaders of Jesus' day, Pharisees, Sadducees, Roman governor, it was Jesus who was upsetting the people, turning the world upside down. In the same way, we speak of the Kuomintang "making a revolution" in China today, seldom by any chance of the Powers having made the revolution by almost a hundred years of trickery, oppression, and inhumanity. Similarly society may permit an utterly impossible situation to develop in an industry like coal, but the workers who finally in desperation put down tools and fold their arms, they are "the strikers," the cause of the breach of the peace. We need to get our thinking focused right, and to see the rulers of Jewry and Rome, not Jesus, the Powers, not the Chinese Nationalists, selfish employers or a negligent society, not striking workers, as the cause of disturbance in the social order.

---

* "Pacifism and Class War," by A. J. Muste from *Pacifism in the Modern World*, Devere Allen, ed. Right to reprint cleared with Harper and Row, Publishers.

A second assumption underlying much of our thinking is that the violence is solely or chiefly committed by the rebels against oppression, and that this violence constitutes the heart of our problem. However, the basic fact is that the economic, social, political order in which we live was built up largely by violence, is now being extended by violence, and is maintained only by violence. A slight knowledge of history, a glimpse at the armies and navies of the Most Christian Powers, at our police and constabulary, at the militaristic fashion in which practically every attempt of workers to organize is greeted, at Nicaragua or China, will suffice to make the point clear to an unbiased mind.

The foremost task, therefore, of the pacifist in connection with class war is to denounce the violence on which the present system is based and all the evil, material and spiritual, this entails for the masses of men throughout the world, and to exhort all rulers in social, political, industrial life, all who occupy places of privilege, all who are the beneficiaries of the present state of things, to relinquish every attempt to hold on to wealth, position, and power by force, to give up the instruments of violence on which they annually spend billions of wealth produced by the sweat and anguish of the toilers. So long as we are not dealing honestly and adequately with this 90 per cent of our problem there is something ludicrous, and perhaps hypocritical, about our concern over the 10 per cent of violence employed by the rebels against oppression. Can we win the rulers of earth to peaceful methods?

The psychological basis for the use of nonviolent methods is the simple rule that like produces like, kindness provokes kindness, as surely as injustice produces resentment and evil. It is sometimes forgotten by those whose pacifism is a spurious, namby-pamby thing that if one Biblical statement of this rule is "Do good to them that hate you" (an exhortation presumably intended for the capitalist as well as for the laborer), another statement of the same rule is, "They that sow the wind shall reap the whirlwind." You get from the universe what you give, with interest! What if men build a system on violence and injustice, on not doing good to those who hate them nor even to those who meekly obey and toil for them? And persist in this course through centuries of Christian history? And if then the oppressed raise the chant:

> Ye who sowed the wind of sorrow,
> Now the whirlwind you must dare,
> As ye face upon the morrow,
> The advancing Proletaire?

In such a day the pacifist is presumably not absolved from preaching to the rebels that they also shall reap what they sow but assuredly not in such wise as to leave the oppressors safely intrenched in their position, not at the cost of preaching to them in all sternness that "the judgments of the Lord are true and righteous altogether."

As we are stayed from preaching nonviolence to the underdog unless and until we have dealt adequately with the dog who is chewing him up, so also are all those who would support a country in war against another country stayed from preaching nonviolence in principle to labor or to radical movements. Much could be said on this point, but it is perhaps unnecessary to dwell on it here. Suffice it to observe in passing that to one who has had any intimate connection with labor the flutter occasioned in certain breasts by the occasional violence in connection with strikes seems utterly ridiculous, and will continue to seem so until the possessors of these fluttering breasts have sacrificed a great deal more than they already have in order to banish from the earth the horrible monster of international war.

We are not, to pursue the matter a little further, in a moral position to advocate nonviolent methods to labor while we continue to be beneficiaries of the existing order. They who profit by violence, though it be indirectly, unwillingly, and only in a small measure, will always be under suspicion and rightly so of seeking to protect their profits, of being selfishly motivated, if they address pious exhortations to those who suffer by that violence.

Nor can anyone really with good conscience advocate abstention from violence to the masses of labor in revolt, unless he is himself identified in spirit with labor and helping it with all his might to achieve its rights and to realize its ideals. In a world built on violence one must be a revolutionary before one can be a pacifist: in such a world a nonrevolutionary pacifist is a contradiction in terms, a monstrosity. During the war no thorough pacifist in America would have felt justified in exhorting Germany to lay down its arms while saying and doing nothing about America's belligerent activities. We should have recognized instantly the moral absurdity, the implied hypocrisy of such a position. Our duty was to win our own "side" to a "more excellent way." It is a sign of ignorance and lack of realism in our pacifist groups and churches that so many fail to recognize clearly and instantly the same point with regard to the practice of pacifism in social and labor struggles. . . .

Pacifism and Patriotism (1929)*

H. C. Englebrecht

Appearing in the same volume as Muste's essay, "Pacifism and Patriotism" by H. C. Englebrecht confronts the patriotic challenge to pacifism head on. It is not written in the friendly manner of the Quakers or the "passive" pacifist but is a fiercely effective polemic, ridiculing and attacking the nationalism which often underlies wars (and had not yet begun to wreak its greatest mischief when Englebrecht wrote).

At the time he composed the essay excerpted here, Engelbrecht was associated with the Federal Council of Churches which he and others influenced in a pacifist direction. During the 1930's, several member churches held referenda on the question of peace which usually resulted in indictments of war.

A rioting New York mob attacked the house of a prominent abolitionist in 1834. It gained an entry and in fierce glee began its work of destruction. Everything movable was thrown out of the windows, drenched in oil, and got ready for a huge bonfire, whose flames somehow were to purge the city of the stain of antislavery agitation. One of the gangsters tore a picture from the wall and was about to commit it to the cleansing fires when he discovered that it was a portrait of George Washington. He hugged it to his breast and shouted dramatically: "It's Washington! For God's sake don't burn Washington!" His cry was immediately echoed in the street: "For God's sake don't burn Washington!" Very tenderly the painting was taken down the stairs and a group of bullies installed it on the veranda of the neighboring house and placed it under careful guard. From his exalted position the Father of the Country looked down on the frenzy of the patriotic vandals.

This little incident illustrates the problem of patriotism. It is an astonishing, often most irrational power, attracting strange pilgrims to its shrine. Its spokesmen proclaim weird doctrines. And what deeds are done in its name! Enormous reserves of oil are stolen by millionaire thieves and a "faithless public servant"—in the name of patriotism. Blacklists, including the best element of the country, are spread—in the name of patriotism. A mayor puts his name on the front page of newspapers on two continents by organizing a "society for hating the British"—in the name of patriotism. Men are insulted on the street for not removing their hats when a military parade passes with the

---

* From *Pacifism in the Modern World*, Devere Allen, ed. Right to reprint cleared with Harper and Row, Publishers.

flag—in the name of patriotism. Women kneel and kiss the Liberty Bell—in the name of patriotism. Children every morning are put through a solemn ritual including a pledge of loyalty and a salute to the flag—in the name of patriotism. There is a journal, fortunately obscure, called *The Patriot*, which sees as its highest duty the vicious denunciation of the Jews. And there is the superpatriotic Ku Klux Klan. Autos are raced over treacherous beaches at death-defying speed to bring back records held abroad—in the name of patriotism. Millions of men are torn from their homes and labors and sent out to fight to the death with other millions whom they do not even know—in the name of patriotism.

Is it any wonder that many cannot speak the word "patriotism" without a sneer? Old Sam Johnson's vigorous judgment that "patriotism is the last refuge of a scoundrel," despite its uncounted repetition, does not seem to stale. Schopenhauer's statement that "patriotism is the passion of fools and the most foolish of passions" will also find a ready echo. The word "patriotism" has fallen from its high estate. It is used so often as a synonym of narrow-mindedness, exclusiveness, fanaticism, selfishness, and bottomless ignorance that intelligent people who sincerely love their country hesitate to apply it to themselves, while cynics employ it as a term of scorn. Whether or not a pacifist may be a patriot depends entirely on what patriotism is.

The pacifist can never be a purely emotional patriot. Flag-waving, parading, cheering, throwing tons of ticker tape on a "hero," Fourth-of-Julying, are not enough. This sort of thing generally lives side by side with profound ignorance and bigotry. It makes saints of Washington and Lincoln and attributes an almost magic significance to being born in a log cabin or rising from the lowly estate of newsboy. It ascribes the greatness of the country to soldiers and bankers. It revels in fierce hatreds, changing the object of detestation readily under the barrage of newspaper propaganda. Every good American used to hate the British, then he turned on the Germans, then on the Russians; meanwhile others have specialized in despising the French or the Japanese or the Southern Europeans.

The pacifist, furthermore, cannot join in any immoral patriotism. Stephen Decatur's "My country, right or wrong!" is probably the most immoral sentence in the language. It makes the state a god, promulgating not only law, but ethics. The pacifist would insist that the state is not outside of the moral categories, but that it is bound by them. Its treaties are not scraps of paper to be torn up at will. Its promises to subject peoples or to colonies must be kept. The liberties of smaller nations dare not be destroyed or their rights invaded whenever the stronger powers find it to their advantage.

Above all, though, the pacifist is not a military patriot. Perhaps this is the heart of the problem. For a great multitude militarism and patriotism are synonymous. The argument is very simple. The country must see to its security. This is possible only by military force. Hence, the true patriot is also a militarist. This argument of necessity is generally adorned with a catalog of the virtues fostered by war. We have not yet forgotten the last war and how the great slaughter was justified and glorified by the leaders in all countries. When the inhuman submarine was bitterly attacked, one preacher declared:

> Submarines are certainly loveless and un-Christian. They are as unrighteous as Mammon. But we use them exactly as Jesus also told us to use Mammon. That is the wonderful thing, that in all these matters we have the words of Jesus on our side.

Again, when the peoples, horrified by the slaughter, were seeking peace, another preacher declared:

> I cannot abide the whining and yammering over the agony and misery of war. War is not a misfortune, but a great good fortune. God be praised that the war came.... And God be praised that we have as yet no peace.... War is the great knife by which God is operating as a mighty surgeon on this people and cutting away the poisonous boils which have been infecting us. God be praised we have as yet no peace!

With all this justification of war and its religious exaltation the pacifist disagrees most strongly. Did military and naval preparedness, never so highly developed as in 1914, make for peace and insure security? The pacifist does not believe that the savage killings, poisoning, maiming, crippling of millions in each country can ever be justified. Even if war really brought permanent settlement of vexing problems— which it does not—it is a procedure utterly unworthy of a reasonable human being. Few men owed as much to war as did Napoleon, yet that vain little soldier was compelled to admit:

> War is an anachronism. Someday victories will be won without cannons and bayonets.... Do you know what I marvel at most in the world? The impotence of force in organization. There are only two powers in the world, the mind and the sword. In the long run the sword is always defeated by the mind.

So the pacifist will have nothing of military patriotism. In this point he will exercise the right of conscience, the right of personal conviction, and dissent. The government may jail him or even worse, but it cannot compel him to violate his conscience and help slaughter in war. For that reason the pacifist is also opposed to all military and naval preparedness. Armies and navies, reserve officers' training corps, citizens' military training camps, are all part of the war system, which the pacifist wishes to see abolished. . . .

On Pilgrimage (1965)*

Dorothy Day

The Catholic Worker Movement is an almost incredible anomaly. It teaches a gentle anarchism and voluntary poverty within the most highly structured and richest church in the world. To the selfless workers in the cause, however, there is nothing incongruous in their actions. They find ample basis for their anarchism and certainly for their voluntary poverty in Roman Catholic traditions. They are emphatically Catholic, accepting even the Church's hierarchical authority. "If the Chancery ordered me to stop publishing the *Catholic Worker* tomorrow," Dorothy Day once said, "I would."

The organization and the woman whose name is intimately associated with it, Dorothy Day, are best known for their work among the most completely outcast of American society, the skid row derelicts. Unlike other organizations engaged in such charity, however, the *Catholic Worker* Movement is concerned with social as well as personal regeneration.

The reading below, from Dorothy Day's regular column in the *Catholic Worker* titled, "On Pilgrimage," provides a fair sampling of her thoughts on war and also the unique character of the newspaper. Distinguished by its humbly low price (1¢ a copy, 25¢ a year), the *Catholic Worker* includes often excellent woodcuts and the startling juxtaposition in its columns of erudite articles on theology and homey gossip.

One wakes early in the city on hot summer mornings, and this morning I began my day by going on with my reading of Pope John XXIII's *Journal of a Soul.* I had reached page 84, "Notes made during the spiritual exercises after the Babylonian Captivity" (which is what he termed his time in the Army). He wrote of knowing what hell was like, now that he had lived in barracks.

---

* Reprinted by permission from the *Catholic Worker* (July–August, 1965).

What blasphemies there were in that place, and what filth. Would
hell be any better? What if I were to end there, while my fellow
soldiers, the poor wretches, who grew up surrounded by evil were
to Paradise—no wonder I tremble at the thought.... O the world
is so ugly, filthy and loathsome! In my year of military service I
have learned all about it. The army is a running fountain of
pollution, enough to submerge whole cities. Who can hope to
escape from this flood of slime, unless God comes to his aid?

In his letters to the rector of the seminary at Rome, young Roncalli
is far more moderate in his expressions; the editorial note which intro-
duces the two letters explains that at that time there were no military
chaplains to give spiritual assistance in the barracks and that his
letters, while commending the courtesy of the officer in command and
the good nature of the Italian soldier, bear out what he wrote in his
notes

with all the frankness of an innocent soul brought face to face
with the reality of the moral crisis in which most young men,
especially those who live the communal life of the barracks, find
themselves involved. In such circumstances the weaker and less
noble, one might say the most melancholy characteristics of youth
come to the fore.

"Nevertheless," young Angello Roncalli wrote, "every day I am
more convinced of the great benefit I shall draw from this year's
experience, for the glory of God and to the advantage of the Church."

Now, half a century later, the Vatican Council at Rome is taking
up this issue of war and peace, and the rights of conscience, as well as
the formation of conscience in regard to the means used in modern war.

There was still time this morning to read a chapter in the Gospel,
and I opened to the 22nd chapter of Luke, which begins with the story
of the Last Supper, Jesus' taking bread and wine and saying: "This is
My Body, this is My Blood," and crying out: "Behold, the hand of
him who betrays Me is with Me on the table."

... And they began to question one another which of them it was
that would do this. A dispute also arose among them which of
them was to be regarded as the greatest.

And He said to them, the kings of the Gentiles lord it over
them; and they that have power over them, are called beneficent.
[The newest version says "Benefactors"—D.D.] But you, not so:
but he that is the greater among you, let him become as the
younger; and he that is the leader, as he that serveth. For which
is greater, he that sitteth at table or he that serveth. Is is not the

one who sits at table? But I am among you as one who serves. And you are those who have continued with me in my trials. And I dispose to you, as my Father hath disposed to me, a kingdom. ... And turning to Simon He rebuked him saying, "Simon, Simon, behold Satan hath desired to have you, that he may sift you as wheat. But I have prayed for thee that thy faith fail not. And thou being once converted, confirm thy brethren." ...

I thought about these very mysterious passages in the half hour I stayed in church after my communion. Often I have thought of how the apostles were afraid and hid themselves behind locked doors. And I thought too of how even after Jesus' death and resurrection they were still hankering after a kingdom, a worldly kingdom and the subjugation of their enemies. It is all there in the pages of the New Testament, in the Gospels and in the Acts of the Apostles. It is not easy reading, the New Testament, any more than the Old is.

.   .   .   .

Certainly Jesus knew that since He was reputed among the wicked, He was always going to be entangled with the things of this world. Christ is our head and we are His members. We are other Christs by our incorporation into the body of Christ. We involve Him even in our sin. "He became sin for us," according to St. Paul. He knew we were going to go after material things. (A certain amount of goods is necessary to lead a good life, St. Thomas Aquinas said.) When the Jews fled Egypt they took with them (as restitution for unpaid wages?) the belongings, the gold and silver of the Egyptians. To this day we have an increase of wealth in the Church until persecution takes it from us, or until we voluntarily do penance, deprive ourselves, deny ourselves and follow Him in serving our brothers. To this day we have the sword and the spectacle of brother fighting against brother, German and Italian Catholic against French and English and American —Catholic, Protestant, Orthodox, fighting each other. "The time will come when you will think you are serving God in putting one another to death."

It is as though He said, "Very well, take your scrip, your purse, your sword. Each one of you must have a personal encounter with Me, your risen Lord, your Jesus, your Master before you understand." Just as Mary Magdalene, Thomas, Peter, James and John did. "I have loved you with an everlasting love even when you are denying Me. You will each one of you, loved uniquely by the Father, have to be visited by the Holy Spirit before you will understand. You have your freedom to make your choices. It is a matter of your individual conscience, your individual conversion. Ask and you will receive. Seek and you will find."

My comfort is that a thousand years are one day in the sight of God, and so Christianity is two days old, we have scarcely begun, we are still defending God and Country (putting them on an equality) by our wealth and our weapons.

Our prayer and our hope is that from the chair of Peter, from the College of Cardinals will come during this last session of the Council, a clear statement, "Put up thy sword," with the healing touch of Jesus in such a statement to the ears of those who, hearing, do not understand.

The apostles didn't take the sword, they cowered in fear instead and could scarcely believe that they saw Him again. They were still asking Him about when the earthly kingdom would come despite His clear statement that His kingdom was not of this world which is a testing ground, a place of trial, a school of Christ, as St. Benedict had it.

But after the Holy Spirit enlightened the apostles they went to martyrdom, embraced the cross, laid down their own lives for their neighbors, in whom they were beginning to see Christ.

"Inasmuch as ye have done it unto one of the least of these my brethren you have done it unto me."

We long with all our hearts for such a statement from the Bishops, clear, uncompromising, courageous. We know that men in their weakness, like the apostles, will still take the sword, will still be denying Christ in their brother the Negro, the Vietnamese.

But the teaching of Jesus has indeed been answered again and again over the ages, from the apostles to the present day and again and again these called by the Holy Spirit and touched by grace have laid down their lives for the faith that God is our Father and all men are our brothers.

. . . .

Christ is being martyred today in Vietnam, in Santo Domingo and in all places where men are taking to the sword in this world crisis. He will be crucified to the end of time. He is with us in His humanity until the end of time.

One of our Catholic pacifists asked me to write a clear, theoretical, logical, pacifist manifesto, and he added so far, in these thirty-three years of *The Catholic Worker*, none had appeared from my pen.

I can write no other than this: Unless we use the weapons of the spirit, denying ourselves and taking up our cross and following Jesus, dying with Him and rising with Him, men will go on fighting, and often from the highest motives, believing that they are fighting defensive wars for justice for others and in self-defense against present or future aggression.

To try to stop war by placing before men's eyes the terrible suffering involved will never succeed, because men are willing (in their thoughts and imaginations at least) to face any kind of suffering when motivated by noble aims like the vague and tremendous concept of freedom, God's greatest gift to man, which they may not articulate but merely sense. . . .

This month I saw the film *China!* and two years ago I visited Cuba and saw the changes the Marxist-Leninists were making there. Living so close to misery and vice, destitution and homelessness, hard and cruel labor, sickness of mind and soul and body at the *Catholic Worker* as we do—seeing all this aspect of life each day in city and country, one is tempted by such a vision of a *forcible* working towards the common good.

If the Chinese and the Cubans are working for justice, and a better life for the masses, are they not also working for Christ, though they do not know Him? But as Harold Robbins, the distributist, wrote in *The Sun of Justice:*

> Freedom is the primary and supreme reason for the existence of mankind. That He should be freely loved and served seems, as far as our thought can penetrate, to have been God's chief reason for calling us into being. At the cost of this freedom God could have established and maintained a world full of *order*, but not of justice, for free will is of the essence of human justice.

It is on these grounds that we stand opposed to war, upholding this freedom for Communist and capitalist, the East and the West.

The Jehovah's Witnesses in Prison, 1940–1945*

Mulford Sibley and Ada Wardlaw

The Jehovah's Witnesses were the largest single group of religious objectors to military service during World War II. Comparatively few at the time of the First World War, the Witnesses had grown considerably since and, in large

---

* From "Conscientious Objectors in Prison, 1940–1945," Pacifist Research Bureau pamphlet (October, 1945).

numbers between 1940 and 1945, refused not only induction into the armed forces but any cooperation with conscription. The Witnesses individually claimed exemption as ministers and, when refused this classification, went to prison where they remained aloof from other objectors.

Intrinsically conservative while most objectors were progressives, the Witnesses were also authoritarian among themselves while most C.O.'s were staunchly libertarian. The Witnesses were not really pacifists except in the broadest sense of the term. Their refusal to serve in the armed forces was not based on the traditional concepts of either the universal brotherhood of man or the infinite value of each human life. Rather, the Witnesses held to a complex and apocalyptic view of history quite bizarre to both other objectors and the judges who sentenced them.

Despite their numbers and their desire to "witness" their beliefs, Jehovah's Witnesses as objectors to army or Civilian Public Service induction were little understood, either by the public or by fellow-objectors. Witnesses did not customarily issue individual statements of their position as did many other objectors. Although their publications were numerous and easily available, the peculiar idiom of Witness utterances was discouraging to a generation unused to Biblical literalism and apocalyptic views of life. They professed no general doctrine of abstract pacifism—no theory of violence and non-violence, and no philosophy of ends and means. They were quite willing on occasion to defend themselves by physical force; and their doctrine seemed to imply a willingness to engage in one kind of war, with the aid and approval of Jehovah. Yet anyone who has examined their actions and attitudes during the Second World War can scarcely doubt that most Witnesses were deeply *conscientious*.

However, it is difficult to interpret accurately the position of the Witnesses. High officials of the Watchtower Society, which guided the group, were exceedingly loath to comment upon their position with regard to war resistance. In general, the leaders maintained that there was never an official "J.W." view on the advisability of resistance, and that each individual Witness made his own decision, unaffected by any specific interpretation which might be given by the Society. Individuals were said to be bound only by God's will and not by the wills of earthly ecclesiastical authorities. Yet the whole basis of Witness resistance was so much a part of the general view of life elaborated for them in the teachings of the Watchtower Society, that some effort must be made to examine those doctrines. Filled as they are with countless references to Biblical literature, they constitute a philosophy of history, a doctrine of the elect, and a view of a future.

Although Jehovah's Witnesses regarded themselves as beginning, in modern times, in 1878, their interpretation of Biblical history discovered the first Witness in Abel. Between the time of Abel and that of Noah, Satan and the Lord were pictured as contesting against each other for the souls and bodies of men—so much so that eventually God seemed to be defeated, having only one man of integrity, Noah, left upon earth. Then came the Flood, through which it was demonstrated that even *one* man of integrity with the help of the Lord could subdue the spirits of evil—a demonstration of the power of those who witness for Jehovah. The Flood was symbolical of the world coming to an end, and Noah of a greater Witness who would eventually destroy all evil.

Evil, it appears, was not eliminated after the Flood; it only took different shape. While God continued to send prophecies of a new heaven and a new earth, the reorganization of the kingdom of Satan was reflected in the establishment of human government under Nimrod, the great hunter. The "earth" was now to be identified with the political state, with which priestcraft and "religion"—really demonism —were in firm alliance. Abraham and others carried on the witness for Jehovah; but Satan extended his domain through the "great powers" of the world—Egypt, Assyria, Babylonia, Persia, Greece and first pagan, then papal Rome. The last of these became the connecting link between ancient empires and the modern imperial struggle. The seventh empire to appear was the Anglo-American combination which, wounding the papal–German alliance of 1914–1918, became the "professed champion of democracy" in the Second World War, against the renewed alliance of the papacy with Germany.

Meanwhile, symbols of the future ideal order had arisen from time to time to antagonize the kingdoms of earth. Such men as Moses, David and Solomon represented, however imperfectly, the great Theocracy which God, cooperating with His Witnesses, would finally set up in the new world. But the Israelites, heedless of the word of Jehovah, given through His prophets, became corrupt and God punished them for their misdeeds. After the overthrow of Nineveh, the Times of the Gentiles were initiated. Known also as the "seven times" and each "time" being equivalent, in prophecy, to 360 years, this period was to expire 2,520 years after the fall of Nineveh, or by 1914. In that year, Satan's rule began to decline and the Time of the End was established. For Jehovah's Witnesses, the year 1918 marked the entry of Jesus, the chief Theocratic Servant, into the Temple, where He began to judge which servants of Jehovah should be the leaders in finally ridding the earth of Satan. The propagation of Jehovah's word throughout the earth was then insured. This universal evangelization was believed to be foretold in the New Testament (Matthew 24:14) as the harbinger of the Final End.

After Jesus came into the Temple, there seemed to be a brief respite in the violent political struggles of the world, but Satan was merely girding his loins for another blow. The King of the North mentioned in the prophecy of Daniel was identified with the papacy, which, with its German and Central European Allies, was defeated in the First World War by the King of the South (symbolically, Egypt; on the scene of twentieth century struggle, the alliance of the United States and Great Britain). But no sooner had the defeat come about than the Northern King began to scheme to regain his power. He aided in the destruction of the democracies of Germany and Spain, and when the time was ripe, he struck through his Fascist Allies—in Ethiopia, Spain, Austria and Czechoslovakia—the King of the South giving way in each case. In the end, however, the King of the South counter-attacked and the Second World War was upon the world.

Witnesses agreed that one power symbolized the totalitarian order in the world and another the democratic principle. But democracy was pointed out to be government by creatures, not rule by God the Creator. According to Jehovah's Witnesses, the Second World War was a search for power and dominion by both sides. Certain religious groups supposedly resisting the demands of the King of the North belied their pretenses by supporting the King of the South, whose purpose, too, was world domination and opposition to the Witnesses of Jehovah. Some of the Witnesses might give way during this period of trial and tribulation; but the faithful few, loyal to the eventual coming of the Theocratic Government, would follow neither the King of the North nor the King of the South. They remained Witnesses of Jehovah.

Looking into the future they pictured as the end of the struggle the establishment of a "world federation" in which the Northern and Southern Kings would pool their resources and, thus jointly achieving the goal of world domination, would so harry and persecute the Witnesses of Jehovah as to make open proclamation of the day of the Lord impossible. But no sooner would the worldly power have achieved this apparent triumph than, fulfilling Daniel's prophecy (Daniel 11:44), Christ Jesus would announce in a loud voice that the final end was at hand. Then would the battle of Armageddon be fought, the Witnesses of Jehovah emerge triumphant with the Lord, and the New World be born. The Theocracy of the Lord would reign supreme throughout the earth, and all man's domination vanish forever.

Something like this, then, is the framework of thought which Jehovah's Witnesses took with them to prison. As zealots in a crusade far above the claims of nationalism, they accepted prison cheerfully, for the most part, not only in the United States but throughout the warring world. They constituted a large segment of all those in German concentration camps; and in Canada their publications were forbidden as a measure of wartime policy.

But why, in the United States, did they refuse in such large numbers to enter Civilian Public Service camps when granted the status of Conscientious Objectors? Jehovah's Witnesses possess an intense sense of mission, an unwavering belief in the necessity of proclaiming the imminent Time of the End. Their apocalyptic vision was vividly portrayed and amazingly appealing to a large number of men and women who found themselves lost in the seeming utter chaos of the modern world. Young Witnesses reached the conclusions that it was their duty to agree to no service which would interfere with their witnessing. To them the preaching of their message on street corners and its propagation by means of phonograph records in house-to-house calls was the task to which they were supremely summoned. Whatever their occupation might be—mechanics, artisans, farmers, clerks—they regarded themselves primarily as preachers of the coming Armageddon. Others were so eager to do the Lord's work that they gave up all worldly tasks for the full-time mission of preaching.

Thus when they came before the local Selective Service Boards, they demanded classification as ministers (IV-D), which would have given them total exemption. Some Local Boards refused to recognize them as ministers, which in view of the unusual nature of Jehovah's Witnesses and the hostility of public opinion to them in many communities, is not surprising. In many instances the evidence was overwhelming that the Witnesses were engaged in ministerial work for a total of more than the eighty hours a month which the Director of Selective Service set as a minimum for classification as ministers. In some few cases, it was quite clear that Local Boards and Appeal Boards ignored the claim of Witnesses who were spending all their time as ministers. There was no appeal to the courts unless they first reported to the Army or Civilian Public Service, as the case might be, and then attempted to get release on a writ of *habeas corpus*. To do this would have meant for many Witnesses a surrender of their most cherished convictions.

Representative of perhaps hundreds who refused to obey orders to report to Army or CPS was the letter of one Witness to his Local Board explaining why he found himself unable to comply with its order:

You have determined upon a course of action. Your decision,
I hope has been well considered. As for me, I will continue to
perform my obligations as a servant of Jehovah. This will require
of me uncompromising devotion to the Kingdom for which all
true Christians pray. I cannot as a Christian comply with your
order to appear for military service. This is not in defiance of
you but in obedience to God's command.

It little matters the consequences to me, for I know that I
have followed good conscience and the Scriptures. The main consideration is that I may be regarded with favor by the Supreme
Judge. If it is necessary for me to suffer as a result of my determined course, I will consider it a privilege. "For even hereunto
were ye called; because Christ also suffered for us, leaving us an
example, that ye should follow His steps." (I Pet. 2:21.)

For the Jehovah's Witness, then, the primary reason for violating
the law was not opposition to war, but opposition to any restrictions
on his preaching. This did not mean he was not also opposed to the
Second World War, viewing it as he did in the light of his theology,
but rather that he gave precedence to the vocational aspect of his
resistance. The proclamation of the end of the world was an imperative
with which no human authority had the right to interfere, whether in
war or in peace.

That Men May Live (1967)

The Fellowship of Reconciliation

While World War I virtually destroyed the nineteenth-century peace organizations, it created new and far more vital ones. The Fellowship of Reconciliation
has been the most significant. It was founded in England shortly after the outbreak of war by Henry Hodgkin, a Quaker and friend of Kaiser William II's pacifist
chaplain, Friedrich Siegmund-Schultze, who was arrested twenty-seven times
during World War I. It is an international organization and the leading American
pacifist organization. Its principles, expressed succinctly in a leaflet, "That Men
May Live in Peace Together," are here reproduced.

The Fellowship of Reconciliation is composed of men and women
who recognize the essential unity of mankind and have joined together
to explore the power of love and truth for resolving human conflict.

While it has always been vigorous in its opposition to war, the Fellowship has insisted equally that this effort must be rooted in a commitment to the achieving of a peaceful world community. Thus international peace is not the only objective of the Fellowship: it sees war as the consequence and manifestation of the brokenness of community, while it recognizes peace as the fruit and pleasure of a community that cherishes and defends the full dignity and freedom of every human being everywhere.

In the working out of such objectives the Fellowship seeks the company of those of whatever faith who wish to confront human differences with nonviolent, compassionate and reconciling love. The Fellowship began as a movement of protest against war, with its roots in the ethic of love as found preeminently in Jesus Christ. Many of its members today are motivated by a commitment to God as revealed in Jesus Christ, and to a life of obedience to Christ as Lord. The participation of others is nourished in the historic faith and community of Judaism, with its prophetic emphases on universalism, justice, and love. Still others affirm their faith in man and in the unity and interdependence of the human race, and their intent that life shall be made truly human.

Any requirement of credal uniformity thus is alien to the spirit of the Fellowship; its diversity of motivation is the source of neither embarrassment nor dilution, but of strength and assurance. The Fellowship seeks to demonstrate the integration of faith and life for which religion at its best exists, and to do it within a framework of respect for the integrity of each member's personal beliefs. It is a special role of the Fellowship to extend the boundaries of community in radical directions, as it seeks the resolution of cultural conflicts by the united efforts of men of many faiths.

In the development of its program, the Fellowship does not depend upon a large number of nominal adherents, but upon persons who, accepting its principles fully for themselves, will give time individually and in groups to the application to those principles to every area of life. Although members do not bind themselves to any exact form of words—

1) They identify with those of every nation, race and religion who are the victims of injustice and exploitation, and seek to develop resources of active nonviolent intervention with which to help rescue them from such circumstances;

2) They work to abolish war and to create a community of concern transcending all national boundaries and selfish interests; as an integral part of that commitment they refuse

to participate personally in any war, or to give any sanction they can withhold from physical, moral or psychological preparation for war;

3) They strive to build a social order that will utilize the resources of human ingenuity and wisdom for the benefit of all men, and in which no individual or group will be exploited or oppressed for the profit or pleasure of others;

4) They advocate methods of dealing with offenders against society that will be founded on understanding and forgiveness, and that will seek to redeem and rehabilitate the offender rather than impose punishment on him;

5) They endeavor to show reverence for personality—in the home, in vocational relationships, in school and the processes of education, in association with persons of other racial, credal or national backgrounds;

6) They seek to avoid bitterness and contention in dealing with controversy, and to maintain the spirit of self-giving love while engaged in the effort to achieve these purposes.

The Fellowship's unity is of those who share a common vision and a common task: the vision is of a just and peaceful world; the task is nothing less than the permeation of the whole process of social change with the spirit of human kinship.

Chapter Two:

Opponents of Wars

The Colonial Period

Absolute pacifists have never been more than a tiny minority in the United States. They have, however, periodically found allies among men and women who believe war sometimes justifiable but have opposed specific American conflicts for any of a variety of reasons. Some have seen the United States as the aggressor in particular wars. Others have thought the American cause unjust, American methods brutal or otherwise criminal, or simply viewed certain wars as inexpedient.

Perhaps the earliest non-pacifist opponent of an American war was Roger Williams (c. 1603–1683), the cantankerous Puritan divine who founded the colony of Rhode Island. Williams was serving as minister to churches in Plymouth and Salem when he publicly denied the right of the civil government to enforce religious tenets and maintained that the colony's land was legally the property of the Indians.

It was Williams' attitude toward the Indians which made him an opponent of war, for he did not acknowledge Puritan ownership of Massachusetts Bay by right of conquest. The men of Massachusetts were neither more nor less brutal toward the Indians than the other European settlers of North America. But they were, because of their theological bent, particularly sensitive on the question. They required scriptural justification for all their actions and sanctioned bloody slaughters of the aborigines on the contrived grounds that the Indians were children of Satan in whose extirpation a dour God rejoiced.

Williams scoffed at such reasoning and inveighed against the murder of innocents as a gross immorality. Williams insisted that the Indians owned North America by virtue of their occupation and that the English must purchase the land if they were legally to settle it. Therefore, Williams concluded, the King's grants to the Puritans were spurious, of no value whatsoever. He could not grant what he did not own. Williams' arguments were not calculated to endear Massachusetts Bay to an already suspicious King. Moreover, he was striking at the heart of the Puritans' covenant theology which regarded contracts, including even colonial charters, as inviolable. He was expelled from the colony.

No such worthy principles motivated the sentiment in opposition to the series of colonial wars with the French which commenced formally in 1689. There was no *movement* as such. But King William's War (1689–1697), Queen Anne's War (1702–1713), King George's War (1740–1748), and even the French and Indian War (1754–1763) were received in the colonies with a great deal of popular distaste and even more indifference.

Already acting like a new nationality, if not thinking of themselves as one, many colonists viewed the wars as essentially European conflicts that unnecessarily involved their own frontiers and waters. An ill-fated agreement of Louis XIV and James II (1686) to declare the western hemisphere off limits in their wars reinforced this reasoning.

Colonial indifference to the wars was most pronounced in Pennsylvania's reluctance to contribute to the war effort. In other colonies, British generals complained of the indifference of the colonists and their inefficiency as soldiers. Some colonists traded freely with French and Indians who, in other parts, were doing battle with British regulars and colonial militia. The colonial indifference was not organized (and in some areas, like New England, the wars were prosecuted ferociously) but, in the sense that the colonial attitude affected the war effort, it may be reckoned as a significant influence.

Only with their Revolution did large numbers of Americans first oppose a war actively. Many colonists rallied to the British standards or passively assisted the British cause. An even larger number of colonists were quite indifferent to both sides. Firm resolution characterized those who risked their "lives, fortunes, and sacred honor" for the cause of independence. But many colonials were simply confused by the issues at stake; they looked askance at a movement which vilified the King, no matter how much they might resent British policies.

The Young Nation

Anti-war sentiment reached similar proportions during the second war with Great Britain, the War of 1812. It centered in New England and was based on the war's disruption of New England's lifeline, trade. Throughout the first decade of the nineteenth century, the Republican governments of Thomas Jefferson and James Madison had attempted to deal with British depredations against American merchant ships by restricting American trade. New England shippers indeed resented British seizure of ships and impressment of American seamen. But they resented even more sorely the restriction of their trade when war in Europe promised high profits for shippers. When Madison declared war against Great Britain in 1812, it was the last straw. New Englanders viewed "Mr. Madison's War" as the irresponsible work of westerners hungry for Indian and Canadian lands.

Militarily the war was a disaster. American naval forces held their own on the Atlantic and Lake Erie but British troops invaded the United States and put the torch to the national capital. American expeditions to conquer Canada turned into fiascos. As the course of the war worsened, anti-war sentiment grew. New England ministers thundered against the war from their pulpits, bankers were pressured not to loan money to the war effort, and several New England states refused to permit their militia to leave the states.

New England was also the center of widespread opposition to the Mexican War which broke out in 1845. The immediate origin of the war was the establishment of the Republic of Texas by American colonists in the former Mexican province. Most Texans were uninterested in maintaining the independence of the "Lone Star Republic"; they wanted to be admitted to the union as a state and the expansionist administrations of John Tyler and James Polk were anxious to oblige them. Anti-slavery forces, which disliked the prospect of another slave state, forestalled the annexation of Texas by treaty, but, by parliamentary ploy, the expansionists won the day.

The United States' new boundary with Mexico was disputed and, with troops soon in the area, border incidents were not long in coming. American expansionists welcomed the imminent war as an opportunity to detach more land from Mexico.

The movement in opposition to the war was motivated primarily by anti-slavery feelings. Abolitionists and Free Soilers saw the war as a slaveholders' conspiracy to add to the Union Mexican lands they thought suitable for slave agriculture. They also chided the United States for bullying a weak and divided neighbor. The hostility to the war was centered in New England but significant also in the Midwest. Congressman Abraham Lincoln first came to national attention as an anti-war Whig who challenged the administration to show the spot on the map where, it was alleged, Mexican troops had attacked Americans on American soil. The implication was that the government fabricated the incidents. Lincoln was defeated for re-election.

The Civil War

Opposition to the American Civil War was widespread but, inherent to the civil nature of the conflict, technically *fifth columnist*. Not all, however. Many men, Union and Confederate, were not partisan to the enemy's cause but opposed the war on grounds, for example, that any fratricidal war was inherently evil. The Democratic Party platform for 1864 called for a compromise peace. The candidate, George B. McClellan (1826–1885), formally repudiated the plank but banked on northern anti-war sentiment to elect him.

Much northern anti-war feeling was rooted in political partisanship. Northern Democrats could not help but feel uncomfortable in alliance with Republicans in a war against their former political allies. Local issues, defeatism, and opposition to the North's goal of abolition also aroused anti-war feeling. The greatest single outburst occurred in mid-July, 1863, in New York City, where Irish workingmen rioted for half a week in protest against conscription. The rioters viewed the Conscription Act as inequitable: a rich man could escape the draft by hiring a substitute, a poor man simply had to fight. In addition, the men's racism was exacerbated by a fear that freed slaves would swarm into northern cities and steal the manual jobs of the Irish immigrants. The riot was destructive of both life and property but was finally subdued and marked the last major outbreak in the North.

In the South the war was widely disliked. As with the Union armies, the desertion rate was high (about 10 per cent). Many southern conservatives—most of them old Whigs—could not conceive of a viable South independent of the North. The extent of their distaste was revealed only after the war, however. During the conflict, most southern Unionists did not actively agitate for peace; many actually accepted positions in the Confederate government and others quietly sat out the duration at home.

Anti-Imperialism

The Spanish-American War did not last long enough for a substantial anti-war movement to develop. But there was long-standing opposition to the imperialism and navalism which led up to it. Anti-imperialism cut deep in American politics. Attempts to annex Hawaii to the United States had been frustrated for a decade, and the post-war annexation of the Philippines might also have been avoided had it not been for the strange political reasoning of anti-imperialist, William Jennings Bryan (1860–1925). The unofficial leader of the Democratic Party, Bryan prevailed on the party to acquiesce in the annexation of the Philippines so that the party could base its 1900 campaign on an anti-annexation platform. The party did and, led by Bryan, lost the election.

American anti-imperialism was based in part on the fact that the United States had been born in a colonial struggle, that it was a mockery of American principles for the nation to fasten its controls on other peoples. Anti-imperialists also repeated the admonition of the Mexican War that it was unseemly for the United States to pick fights with weak nations.

Anti-imperialism went hand-in-hand with anti-navalism. Inspired by naval theorist Alfred Mahan (1840–1914) and steel manufacturers eager for government contracts, the United States built in the late nineteenth century a huge navy. Anti-navalists mocked the ludicrous aspects of the program. They pointed out, for example, that battleships which rolled from the ways, sometimes at the rate of two a year, were obsolete before they hit the water. They were far inferior to their German and British equivalents and could not even keep up with the rest of the inefficient American fleet. But the implications of the big navy movement seemed more sinister than ludicrous, indicating a trend toward the militarism traditionally thought dangerous to democratic institutions.

Just as pacifism prospered during the first decade of the twentieth century, anti-imperialism was a powerful if not determinant movement. In fact, the pacifist movement was largely swallowed up by the anti-imperialists. While economic arguments were deemphasized, the humanitarian impulse was stimulated by reports from the Philippines of American atrocities which quite rivaled the Spanish record in Cuba. But the imperialists had their way as the United States continued to intervene at will in Cuba, Haiti, Santo Domingo, Nicaragua, and Mexico.

The First World War

Non-pacifist opposition to World War I was considerable and took many forms. Before the actual American entrance into the war, in fact, a majority of Americans seemed determined to keep out of the bloody conflict. They regarded the war as but another evidence of European society's corruption and were thankful for their own geographical isolation from the Continent. Much of this sentiment endured beyond Germany's offensive policy of unrestricted submarine warfare and the efforts of pro-war "preparedness" committees to whip up enthusiasm for the war.

When the United States did enter the war, the majority of Americans lined up behind the war effort or passively accepted the government's action. But significant groups did not. Among Irish-Americans, for example, there was some chagrin at the prospect of a war on the side of hated England. German-Americans and emigrants from the Austro-Hungarian Empire were also dismayed at the prospect of war with their mother countries. The war was never accepted in areas like rural Wisconsin where German immigrants were numerous.

But the most active anti-war organization was motivated by ideological rather than ethnic considerations. The Socialist Party of America was then a significant force in American politics. Immediately after the United States entered the war, the party met in emergency convention at St. Louis and declared its unequivocal opposition. The party prospered at the polls for its stand; a great many Americans obviously agreed with the party's anti-war stand if not necessarily with its economic program. But the party also suffered. Victor Berger, elected to Congress from the city of Milwaukee, was denied his seat because of his anti-war stand, elected again at a special election and again refused. Socialist members of the New York Legislature were expelled from that body. And Eugene V. Debs, the symbolic leader of the party, was sentenced in 1918 to Atlanta Penitentiary for an anti-war speech; he ran for president from his cell in 1920.

Another left-wing organization which suffered from governmental repression was the Industrial Workers of the World, a revolutionary labor union.* Ironically, the IWW was by no means a leader in the anti-war campaign. The "Wobblies" (as members of the IWW were called) did, as good internationalists, condemn the nationalistic war and, as socialists, condemned it as a "rich man's war and poor man's fight." But the IWW concluded that it had no hope of influencing government policies and elected to speak on the issue as quietly as possible, concentrating on labor union goals and hoping that the union would emerge unscathed. Militant opposition to the war, IWW leaders like Big Bill Haywood (1869–1927) reasoned, would only invite governmental suppression at a time

---

* For a more detailed discussion of the IWW and the radical labor movement, see *Ferment in Labor*, another Insight Series book, by Jerome Wolf.

when the union was beginning to prosper. The union's policy was no use. The government moved against the IWW with an ardor it never displayed against the Socialists. In a series of trials, the union's leaders were sentenced to disproportionately long jail terms and their absence from the union for several years fatally crippled the organization.

Finally, more "respectable" Americans quite within the mainstream of American politics actively opposed the war in at least its early stages. Prominent United States senators like Robert M. La Follette of Wisconsin (1855–1925) and George Norris of Nebraska (1861–1944) voted against the declaration of war and delivered speeches against it.

The Second World War and After

The irony of the harsh repression of voices opposed to World War I lay in the fact that within a decade most Americans regarded the intervention as an error never to be repeated. The failure of the war "to make the world safe for democracy" and "to end all wars" disillusioned Americans, as did revelations of the role played by munitions and financial interests in manipulating the country into intervention. Thus, in the months after the outbreak of World War II in September, 1939, American opinion seemed firmly arrayed against the prospect of American participation. Isolationism—preaching defense at home and noninvolvement abroad—was the rule. Between the signing of the Nazi–Soviet pact and Hitler's invasion of Russia, even American Communists lobbied against participating.

The Japanese attack on Pearl Harbor changed the situation almost overnight. Pacifists kept the faith, as did a few small groups such as a splinter of the tiny Socialist Workers Party. But the reality of an attack on the United States swept away virtually every other objection. No previous American war had been so broadly supported.

The situation changed little during the immediate post-war period. The Soviet Union appeared increasingly as a threat to the United States. Full scale military preparedness during peacetime, traditionally unpopular, became an accepted part of American life. A huge standing army was maintained through the establishment of peacetime conscription. Over half of government expenditures was pumped into the war machine. Even the traditional image of the peacetime soldier as an unsavory social misfit was displaced by the image of the cleancut public servant whose sacrifice permitted all to sleep soundly.

Post-war pressures for conformity of thought, moreover, and the devastating power of the political smear—silencing an opponent by alluding to his position as "red"—retarded serious questioning of foreign policy. A citizen was likely to be dubbed a "communist" if he challenged the military, and "communist" was the last word an American of the forties and fifties wished to hear applied to himself.

Thus, when hostilities with North Korean and, later, Chinese troops commenced in 1950, the American anti-war movement stood at its nadir. The "police action" elicited virtually no organized non-pacifist opposition. But the nation found itself in a quandary: while most Americans supported the government's objectives, they were also growing weary of the fighting by 1952. Presidential candidate Dwight D. Eisenhower showed the way out. As a military hero, he could call for an end to the fighting without being labeled a traitor or dupe. Eisenhower also emphasized that he intended no basic alteration of American foreign policy.

The Cold War weakened the peace movement. But the use of atom bombs at Hiroshima and Nagasaki at the end of World War II had provided a new ideological basis for anti-war sentiment in America. The potential of nuclear weapons for absolute annihilation and the publicity given the horrors wreaked by American bombs in Japan convinced some Americans to oppose, if not war itself, the possibility of nuclear war. These were not necessarily pacifists. Many members of the Committee for a Sane Nuclear Policy (SANE), for example, admitted that various past wars had been just and admitted that some future wars might be also. But, they argued, when one spoke of nuclear war, one spoke not "merely" of millions killed but of the very eradication of civilization. Even to consider nuclear war, then, seemed insane.

Groups like SANE agitated for nuclear disarmament and warned against incidents which could lead to a nuclear confrontation. The organization was later criticized for the fact that, during the 1950's, it questioned none of the basic assumptions of American foreign policy except nuclear sabre-rattling. But the fifties were an age of great political apathy in the United States, and in this context, SANE was a very vital force in the anti-war movement.

The resurgence of sizeable anti-war organizations was a phenomenon of the 1960's. The civil rights movement introduced many Americans to political activism and the rhetoric of John F. Kennedy seemed to promise innovation in American life. Interest in the root causes of America's failure to do justice to its large Negro minority led thousands of young idealists to search more deeply into the nature of American society. And the failure of President Kennedy to make any manifest departures from established American foreign policies, dramatized by his approval of the invasion of Cuba in 1961, channeled that probing to an exploration of America's policies abroad. It required only the increasingly obvious American involvement in Vietnam to give birth to an anti-war movement of a size and militance unprecedented in American affairs.

Report of the Hartford Convention (1815)

The War of 1812, ostensibly fought to defend American maritime interests, was actively opposed in New England, the nation's maritime section. In fact, the war was the wish of southern and western warhawks, flexing newly-discovered nationalistic muscles, resentful of British insults, and hungry for land in Canada.

Most of New England's congressmen opposed the declaration of the war and, when war was a fact, several New England states refused to release their militia for anything but defense.

Opposition to the War of 1812 was eminently respectable in New England. Brahmins as conventional as Timothy Pickering and George Cabot discussed secession from the United States as a possible policy. The Hartford Convention, meeting in December and January, 1814–1815, marked the culmination of this movement and, in its final report, circumspectly urged caution on itself. Open resistance to the government's war policy, the convention noted,

> even when justifiable, cannot fail to be painful to the good citizen; and the success of the effort will be no security against the danger of the example. Precedents of resistance to the worst administration, are eagerly seized by those who are naturally hostile to the best. Necessity alone can sanction a resort to this measure; and it should never be extended in duration of degree beyond the exigency.

Nevertheless, it was quite possible that the Hartford Convention would have recommended secession from the Union had not the war been suddenly ended.

New England's opposition to the war was based largely on the fact that it caused widespread destruction of American commerce as the second passage below will illustrate. In addition, however, the New Englanders resented and feared what they interpreted as a drift toward militarism in a nation dedicated against it. The first section here illustrates this as does the third, a proposed amendment to the Constitution.

[I]

Among the subjects of complaint and apprehension, . . . the attention of the convention has been occupied with the claims and pretensions advanced, and the authority exercised over the militia, by the executive and legislative departments of the national government. Also, upon the destitution of the means of defence in which the eastern states are left; while at the same time they are doomed to heavy requisitions of men and money for national objects.

The authority of the national government over the militia is derived from those clauses in the Constitution which give power to Congress "to provide for calling forth the militia to execute the laws of the Union, suppress insurrections and repel invasions";—also "to provide for organizing, arming, and disciplining the militia, and for governing such parts of them as may be employed in the service of the United States, reserving to the states respectively the appointment of the officers, and the authority of training the militia according to the discipline prescribed by Congress." Again, "the President shall be commander in chief of the army and navy of the United States, and of the militia of the several states, *when called into the actual service of the United States.*" In these specified cases only, has the national government any power over the militia; and it follows conclusively that for all general and ordinary purposes this power belongs to the states respectively, and to them alone. It is not only with regret, but with astonishment, the convention preceive that under color of an authority conferred with such plain and precise limitations, a power is arrogated by the executive government, and in some instances sanctioned by the two houses of Congress, of control over the militia, which if conceded will render nugatory the rightful authority of the individual states over that class of men, and by placing at the disposal of the national government the lives and services of the great body of the people, enable it at pleasure to destroy their liberties, and erect a military despotism on the ruins.

. . . .

If the declaration of the president should be admitted to be an unerring test of the existence of these cases, this important power would depend, not upon the truth of the fact, but upon executive infallibility. And the limitation of the power would consequently be nothing more than merely nominal, as it might always be eluded. It follows therefore that the decision of the president in this particular cannot be conclusive. It is as much the duty of the state authorities to watch over the rights *reserved*, as of the United States to exercise the powers which are *delegated*.

The arrangement of the United States into military districts, with a small portion of the regular force, under an officer of high rank of the standing army, with power to call for the militia as circumstances in his judgment may require, and to assume the command of them, is not warranted by the Constitution or any law of the United States. It is not denied that Congress may delegate to the president of the United States the power to call forth the militia in the cases which are within their jurisdiction. But he has no authority to substitute military prefects throughout the Union to use their own discretion in such instances. To station an officer of the Army in a military district, without troops corresponding to his rank, for the purpose of taking command of the militia that may be called into service, is a manifest evasion of that provision of the Constitution which expressly reserves to the states the appointment of the officers of the militia; and the object of detaching such officer cannot be well concluded to be any other than that of superceding the governor or other officers of the militia in their right to command.

The power of dividing the militia of the states into classes, and obliging such classes to furnish, by contrast or draft, able-bodied men to serve for one or more years for the defence of the frontier, is not delegated to Congress. If a claim to draft the militia for one year for such general object be admissible, no limitation can be assigned to it but the discretion of those who make the law. Thus, with a power in Congress to authorize such a draft or conscription, and in the executive to decide conclusively upon the existence and continuance of the emergency, the whole militia may be converted into a standing army disposable at the will of the president of the United States.

The power of compelling the militia and other citizens of the United States, by a forcible draft or conscription, to serve in the regular armies as proposed in a late official letter of the Secretary of War, is not delegated to Congress by the Constitution, and the exercise of it would be not less dangerous to their liberties than hostile to the sovereignty of the states. The effort to deduce this power from the right of raising armies is a flagrant attempt to pervert the sense of the clause in the Constitution which confers that right, and is incompatible with other provisions in that instrument. The armies of the United States have always been raised by contract, never by conscription, and nothing more can be wanting to a government possessing the power thus claimed to enable it to usurp the entire control of the militia, in derogation of the authority of the state, and to convert it by impressment into a standing army.

It may be here remarked, as a circumstance illustrative of the determination of the executive to establish an absolute control over all descriptions of citizens, that the right of impressing seamen into the naval service is expressly asserted by the Secretary of the Navy in a late report. Thus a practice, which in a foreign government has been regarded with great abhorrence by the people, finds advocates among those who have been the loudest to condemn it.

The law authorizing the enlistment of minors and apprentices into the armies of the United States, without the consent of parents and guardians, is also repugnant to the spirit of the Constitution. By a construction of the power to raise armies, as applied by our present rulers, not only persons capable of contracting are liable to be impressed into the army, but those who are under legal disabilities to make contracts are to be invested with the capacity, in order to enable them to annul at pleasure contracts made in their behalf by legal guardians. Such an interference with the municipal laws and rights of the several states could never have been contemplated by the framers of the Constitution. It impairs the salutary control and influence of the parent over his child—the master over his servant—the guardian over his ward—and thus destroys the most important relations in society, so that by the conscription of the father, and the seduction of the son, the power of the executive over all the effective male population of the United States is made complete.

Such are some of the odious features of the novel system proposed by the rulers of a free country, under the limited powers derived from the Constitution. What portion of them will be embraced in acts finally to be passed, it is yet impossible to determine. It is, however, sufficiently alarming to perceive that these projects emanate from the highest authority.

   .   .   .   .

An iron despotism can impose no harder servitude upon the citizen than to force him from his home and his occupation, to wage offensive wars undertaken to gratify the pride or passions of his master. The example of France has recently shown that a cabal of individuals assuming to act in the name of the people may transform the great body of citizens into soldiers and deliver them over into the hands of a single tyrant. No war not held in just abhorrence by the people can require the aid of such stratagems to recruit an army. Had the troops already raised and in great numbers sacrificed upon the frontier of Canada been employed for the defence of the country, and had the millions which have been squandered with shameless profusion been appropriated to their payment to the protection of the coast and to the naval service, there would have been no occasion for unconstitutional expedients.

   .   .   .   .

[II]

The next subject which has occupied the attention of the convention, is the means of defence against the common enemy. This naturally leads to the inquiries whether any expectation can be reasonably entertained that adequate provision for the defence of the eastern states will be made by the national government. Whether the several states can, from their own resources, provide for self-defence and fulfill the requisitions which are to be expected for the national treasury, and generally what course of conduct ought to be adopted by those states in relation to the great object of defence?

Without pausing at present to comment upon the causes of the war, it may be assumed as a truth, officially announced, that to achieve the conquest of Canadian territory and to hold it as a pledge for peace is the deliberate purpose of Administration. This enterprise, commenced at a period when government possessed the advantage of selecting the

time and occasion for making a sudden descent upon an unprepared
enemy, now languishes in the third year of the war. It has been prosecuted with various fortune and occasional brilliancy of exploit, but
without any solid acquisition. The British armies have been recruited
by veteran regiments. Their navy commands Ontario. The American
ranks are thinned by the casualties of war. Recruits are discouraged
by the unpopular character of the contest, and by the uncertainty of
receiving their pay.

In the prosecution of this favorite warfare, Administration have
left the exposed and vulnerable parts of the country destitute of all
efficient means of defence. The main body of the regular Army has
been marched to the frontier. The Navy has been stripped of a great
part of its sailors for the service of the lakes. Meanwhile the enemy
scours the seacoast, blockades our ports, ascends our bays and rivers,
makes actual descents in various and distant places, holds some by
force, and threatens all that are assailable with fire and sword. The
seaboard of four of the New England states, following its curvatures,
presents an extent of more than seven hundred miles, generally occupied
by a compact population and accessible by a naval force, exposing a
mass of people and property to the devastation of the enemy which
bears a great proportion to the residue of the maritime frontier of the
United States. This extensive shore has been exposed to frequent
attacks, repeated contributions, and constant alarms. The regular
forces detached by the national government for its defence are mere
pretexts for placing officers of high rank in command. They are besides
confined to a few places, and are too insignificant in number to be
included in any computation.

These states have thus been left to adopt measures for their own
defence. The militia have been constantly kept on the alert and
harassed by garrison duties and other hardships, while the expenses,
of which the national government decline the reimbursement, threaten
to absorb all the resources of the states. The president of the United
States has refused to consider the expense of the militia detached by
state authority for the indispensable defence of the state, as chargeable
to the Union, on the ground of a refusal by the executive of the state
to place them under the command of officers of the regular Army.
Detachments of militia placed at the disposal of the general government have been dismissed either without pay or with depreciated paper.
The prospect of the ensuing campaign is not enlivened by the promise
of any alleviation of these grievances. From authentic documents,
extorted by necessity from those whose inclination might lead them
to conceal the embarrassments of the government, it is apparent that

the treasury is bankrupt and its credit prostrate. So deplorable is the state of the finances that those who feel for the honor and safety of the country would be willing to conceal the melancholy spectacle if those whose infatuation has produced this state of fiscal concerns had not found themselves compelled to unveil it to public view.

.   .   .   .

It is almost superfluous to state the irresistible inference that these states have no capacity of defraying the expense requisite for their own protection and, at the same time, of discharging the demands of the national treasury.

[III]

The . . . [suggested Constitutional] Amendment proposes to restrict the power of making offensive war. In the consideration of this amendment it is not necessary to inquire into the justice of the present war. But one sentiment now exists in relation to its expediency, and regret for its declaration is nearly universal. No indemnity can ever be attained for this terrible calamity, and its only palliation must be found in obstacles to its future recurrence. Rarely can the state of this country call for or justify offensive war. The genius of our institutions is unfavorable to its successful prosecution; the facility of our situation exempts us from its necessity. In this case, as in the former, those more immediately exposed to its fatal effects are a minority of the nation. The commercial towns, the shores of our seas and rivers, contain the population whose vital interests are most vulnerable by a foreign enemy. Agriculture, indeed, must feel at last, but this appeal to its sensibility comes too late. Again, the immense population which has swarmed into the West, remote from immediate danger, and which is constantly augmenting, will not be averse from the occasional disturbances of the Atlantic states. Thus interest may not unfrequently combine with passion and intrigue to plunge the nation into needless wars and compel it to become a military, rather than a happy and flourishing people. These considerations, which it would be easy to augment, call loudly for the limitation proposed in the amendment.

A Mean and Infamous War (1847)*

Theodore Parker

Theodore Parker (1810–1860), minister and abolitionist, was no pacifist. He aided the escape to Canada of numerous fugitive slaves and secretly supported John Brown's abortive attempt in 1859 to instigate a slave insurrection in the South. He was one of the leading non-pacifist opponents of the Mexican War, attacking it not because war was intrinsically bad but because that particular war was evilly motivated. His fiery indictment of the war, abridged below, was delivered in Boston's historic Faneuil Hall on February 4, 1847.

We are in a war; the signs of war are seen here in Boston. Men needed to hew wood and honestly serve society are marching about your streets; they are learning to kill men, men who never harmed us nor them; learning to kill their brothers. It is a mean and infamous war we are fighting. It is a great boy fighting a little one, and that little one feeble and sick. What makes it worse is, the little boy is in the right, and the big boy is in the wrong, and tells solemn lies to make his side seem right. He wants, besides, to make the small boy pay the expenses of the quarrel.

The friends of the war say, "Mexico has invaded our territory!" When it is shown that it is we who have invaded hers, then it is said, "Aye, but she owes us money." Better say outright, "Mexico has land, and we want to steal it!"

This war is waged for a mean and infamous purpose, for the extension of slavery. It is not enough that there are fifteen slave states, and three million men here who have no legal rights—not so much as the horse and the ox have in Boston; it is not enough that the slave-holders annexed Texas, and made slavery perpetual therein, extending even north of Mason and Dixon's line, covering a territory forty-five times as large as the state of Massachusetts. Oh, no; we must have yet more land to whip Negroes in!

The war had a mean and infamous beginning. It began illegally, unconstitutionally. The Whigs say, "The President made the war." Mr. Webster says so! It went on meanly and infamously. Your Congress lied about it. Do not lay the blame on the Democrats; the Whigs lied just as badly. Your Congress has seldom been so single-mouthed before.

---

* Taken from the speech as reprinted in Arthur and Lila Weinberg (eds.), *Instead of Violence* (New York: Grossman Publishers, 1963).

Why, only sixteen voted against the war, or the lie. I say this war is mean and infamous, all the more because waged by a people calling itself democratic and Christian. . . .

We have come to Faneuil Hall to talk about the War; to work against the war. It is rather late, but better late than never. We have let two opportunities for work pass unemployed. One came while the annexation of Texas was pending. Then was the time to push and be active. Then was the time for Massachusetts and all the North to protest as one man against the extension of slavery. Everybody knew all about the matter, the Democrats and the Whigs. But how few worked against that gross mischief! One noble man lifted up his warning voice . . . [John Quincy Adams]; a man noble in his father—and there he stands in marble; noble in himself—and there he stands yet higher up; and I hope time will show him yet nobler in his son—and there he stands, not in marble, but in man! He talked against it, worked against it, fought against it. But Massachusetts did little. Her tonguey men said little; her handy men did little. Too little could not be done or said. True, we came here to Faneuil Hall and passed resolutions; good resolutions they were, too. Daniel Webster wrote them, it is said. They did the same in the state house; but nothing came of them. They say "Hell is paved with resolutions"; these were of that sort of resolutions, which resolve nothing, because they are of words, not works!

Well, we passed the resolutions; you know who opposed them; who hung back and did nothing—nothing good I mean; quite enough not good. Then we thought all the danger was over; that the resolution settled the matter. But then was the time to confound at once the enemies of your country; to show an even front hostile to slavery.

But the chosen time passed over, and nothing was done. Do not lay the blame on the Democrats; a Whig Senate annexed Texas, and so annexed a war. We ought to have told our delegation in Congress, if Texas were annexed, to come home, and we would breathe upon it and sleep upon it, and then see what to do next. Had our resolutions, taken so warmly here in Faneuil Hall in 1845, been but as warmly worked out, we had now been as terrible to the slave power as the slave power, since extended, now is to us!

Why was it that we did nothing? That is a public secret. Perhaps I ought not to tell it to the people.

The annexation of Texas, a slave territory big as the kingdom of France, would not furl a sail on the ocean; would not stop a mill wheel at Lowell! Men thought so.

That time passed by, and there came another. The government had made war; the Congress voted the dollars, voted the men, voted a lie. Your representative men of Boston voted for all three—the lie, the dollars, and the men; all three, in obedience to the slave power! Let him excuse that to the conscience of his party; it is an easy matter. I do not believe he can excuse it to his own conscience. To the conscience of the world it admits of no excuse. Your President called for volunteers, 50,000 of them. Then came an opportunity such as offers not once in one hundred years, an opportunity to speak for freedom and the rights of mankind! Then was the time for Massachusetts to stand up in the spirit of '76, and say, "We won't send a man, from Cape Ann to Williamstown—not one Yankee man, for this wicked war." Then was the time for your merchants to say, "Not a ship, not a dollar, for this wicked war"; for your manufacturers to say, "We will not make you a cannon, nor a sword, not a kernel of powder, nor a soldier's shirt, for this wicked war." Then was the time for all good men to say, "This is a war for slavery, a mean and infamous war; an aristocratic war, a war against the best interests of mankind. If God please, we will die a thousand times, but never draw blade in this wicked war."

. . . .

That is what a democratic nation, a Christian people ought to have said, ought to have done. But we did not say so; the Bay State did not say so, nor your Governor, nor your merchants, nor your manufacturers, nor your good men; the Governor accepted the President's decree, issued his proclamation calling for soldiers, recommended men to enlist, appealing to their "patriotism" and "humanity."

. . . .

I think there is a good deal to excuse the volunteers. I blame them, for some of them know what they are about. Yet I pity them more, for most of them, I am told, are low, ignorant men; some of them drunken and brutal. From the uproar they make here tonight, arms in their hands, I think what was told me is true! I say, I pity them. They are my brothers; not the less brothers because low and misguided. If they are so needy that they are forced to enlist by poverty, surely I pity them. If they are of good families, and know better, I pity them still more! I blame most the men that have duped the rank and file! I blame the captains and colonels, who will have least of the hardships, most of the pay, and all of the "glory." I blame the men that made the war; the men that make money out of it. I blame the great party men of the land. Did not Mr. Clay say he hoped he could slay a Mexican? Yes, he did; said it on Forefather's Day! Did not Mr. Webster, in the streets of Philadelphia, bid the volunteers, misguided young men, go and uphold the stars of their country? No; he should have said the stripes of his country, for every volunteer to this wicked war, is a stripe on the nation's back! Did not he declare this war unconstitutional, and threaten to impeach the President who made it, and then go and invest a son in it? Has it not been said here, "Our country, howsoever bounded," bounded by robbery or bounded by right lines! Has it not been said, all round, "Our country, right or wrong!"

.   .   .   .

It is time for the people of Massachusetts to instruct their servants in Congress to oppose this war; to refuse all supplies for it; to ask for the recall of the army into our own land. It is time for us to tell them that not an inch of slave territory shall ever be added to the realm. Let us remonstrate; let us petition; let us command. If any class of men have hitherto been remiss, let them come forward now and give us their names—the merchants, the manufacturers, the Whigs and the Democrats. If men love their country better than their party or their purse, now let them show it.

Let us ask the General Court of Massachusetts to cancel every commission which the Governor has given to the officers of the volunteers. Let us ask them to disband the companies not yet mustered into actual service; and then, if you like that, ask them to call a convention of the people of Massachusetts, to see what we shall do in reference to the war; in reference to the annexation of more territory; in reference to the violation of the Constitution.

.   .   .   .

Your President tells us it is treason to talk so! Treason, is it? Treason to discuss a war which the government made, and which the people are made to pay for? If it be treason to speak against the war, what was it to make the war, to ask for 50,000 men and $74 million for the war? Why, if the people cannot discuss the war they have got to fight and to pay for, who under heaven can? Whose business is it, if it is not yours and mine? If my country is in the wrong, and I know it, and hold my peace, then I am guilty of treason, moral treason. Why, a wrong—it is only the threshold of ruin. I would not have my country take the next step. Treason is it, to show that this war is wrong and wicked? Why, what if George III, any time from '75 to '83, had gone down to Parliament and told them it was treason to discuss the war then waging against these colonies! What do you think the Commons would have said? What would the Lords say? Why, that King, foolish as he was, would have been lucky if he had not learned there was a joint in his neck, and, stiff as he bore him, that the people knew how to find it.

I do not believe in killing kings, or any other men; but I do say, in a time when the nation was not in danger, that no British king, for two hundred years past, would have dared call it treason to discuss the war—its cause, its progress, or its termination!

Now is the time to act! Twice we have let the occasion slip; beware of the third time! Let it be infamous for a New England man to enlist; for a New England merchant to loan his dollars, or to let his ships in aid of this wicked war; let it be infamous for a manufacturer to make a cannon, a sword, or a kernel of powder to kill our brothers with, while we all know that they are in the right, and we in the wrong.

The New York City Draft Riots (1863)

When conscription went into effect in New York City in mid-July, 1863, the immediate response was pillaging, beatings, and arson, chiefly the work of working-class Irishmen. The rioting was aimed first against draft offices but then against Negroes and wealthy men who had the misfortune to stumble on the rioters. (And one German community used the opportunity to burn a brothel where an eleven-year-old girl was being held.)

It took nearly a week before the city was restored to order and then only after a detachment of troops from the Union encampment at Gettysburg was dispatched to New York. This account, of the first day's riot, is from the *New York Tribune* of July 14, 1863.

Yesterday morning about ten o'clock the draft in the Eleventh Congressional District of which the headquarters are at the corner of Third Avenue and Forty-sixth Street was resumed pursuant to adjournment. . . . The drawing was actually commenced about half-past ten o'clock, and from seventy-five to one hundred names had been drawn from the wheel and announced, when suddenly the report of a pistol was heard in the street.

This seemed to be the signal for an attack upon the office, for almost upon the instant a perfect shower of brickbats, paving stones, and other missiles, were hurled from the street into the building which, of course, took everybody by surprise. Following the shower of stones came an immense crowd who poured into the office carrying everything

before them . . . The Provost Marshals, Commissioners, surgeon, en-
grossing clerks, with the members of the press effected their escape
by the back door, Captain Jenkins clambering a fence and secreting
himself in the next house until a favorable moment when he made
his way home.

One of the clerks who endeavored to save some of the papers was
seized by the crowd, the papers taken from him by force and torn in
pieces. The mob now had possession of the building. In a few moments
thereafter a man appeared with a can of turpentine, which he poured
on the floor of the office, and, setting fire to it, the room was soon in a
blaze. All the time the mob kept breaking up the pavement and pelting
the police and men attached to the office with stones. . . .

Shortly after eleven o'clock a detachment of the Provost Guard
numbering fifteen and a half files belonging to the Invalid Corps left
the Park Barracks and reached the ground about noon. Upon reaching
Thirty-fourth Street the mob began to surround them, howling, yelling,
and groaning. The guard formed in line between Forty-fourth and
Forty-fifth Streets, but were so closely pressed upon all sides that they
were unable to "order arms." The mob now commenced pushing and
jolting the soldiers and throwing stones at them when Lieutenant Reed,
who was in command of the guard, ordered his men to load, and immediately after gave the order to "fire," when the soldiers poured a volley
into the crowd; but no one, it seems, was hurt. The crowd, who had
retreated a short distance when the firing commenced, quickly rallied,
and closing upon the guard, wrested their arms from their hands and
discharged several of the pieces which had been reloaded, into the
crowd. The soldiers, this disarmed, quickly retreated, but were pursued
by the infuriated throng. . . .

Soon after the defeat of the soldiers a strong squad of police made
their appearance in line of battle. As soon as the mob caught sight of
them they fired a volley of stones; knocking down two of the officers.
The police at once drew their clubs and revolvers, but after a contest
of a few mintues they were also forced to retreat, which they did in
good order until near Fortieth Street, when one of them discharged
his revolver four times into the midst of the throng, shooting a horse
that was attached to a wagon standing on the corner. A rush was made
at once for the officer, who immediately retreated into a store near by,
the people of which at once barred the door and endeavored to give
him protection. The crowd, however, went to the back of the house,
tore down the fence, and rushed into the building, seized the policeman,
knocked him down, and beat him in a fearful manner. . . .

Police Superintendent Kennedy, though in citizen's dress, was observed by the mob who made a rush at him and knocked him headlong into the gutter, when several of the rioters kicked him and beat him dreadfully about the head, face, and body. Some one of his friends who chanced to be near by, recognizing Mr. Kennedy, went to his assistance and succeeded in rescueing him. Mr. Kennedy was taken into a store and thence removed to his residence in a carriage. His injuries, though severe, are not regarded of a fatal character, yet will involve his remaining perfectly quiet for some days.

The rioters were composed of the employees of the several railroad companies, the employees of Brown's iron factory in Sixty-first Street, Taylor's factory in Forty-first Street, Cummin's street contractor, and numerous manufactories in the upper part of the city. The crowd marched through many of the streets in the upper part of the city, compelling laborers in every quarter to knock off work and fall in. . . .

The Streets from Forty-first to Sixty-third and the Avenues were full of knots and throngs of laboring men, some counseling violence at once, others discussing their power to effect anything, many drowning better judgement in frequent potations of ardent spirits.

No one seemed able to tell where the initiatory steps of this movement were taken. In a score of places at once men ceased labor and poured into the streets. . . . The vast crowd swayed to and fro, racing first in this direction, then in that, attacking indiscriminately every well-dressed man. The general cry was, "Down with the rich men." Three gentlemen talking together on Lexington Avenue were set upon and knocked down, narrowly escaping with their lives. . . .

Mr. Andrews of Virginia ascended a shanty opposite the burning ruins, where thousands were assembled. Behind this was an open space of untilled ground occupied by dense masses, when Mr. Andrews proceeded to address:

. . . He said he had lately addressed them at a meeting at the Cooper Institute where he told them Mr. Lincoln wanted to tear the hard-working man from his wife and family and send him to the war. He denounced Mr. Lincoln for his conscription bill, which was in favor of the rich and against the poor man. He called him a Nero and a Caligula for such a measure. . . . He then advised the people to organize to resist the draft and appoint their leader, and, if necessary, he would be their leader. (Uproarious cheering.) . . .

As if by preconcerted action an attack was made upon colored men and boys in every part of the city during the day, crowds of from 100 to 500 persons hunting them like bloodhounds. Several inoffensive colored men were dragged off the city cars and badly beaten, while a number were taken from carts and drays which they were driving and terribly maltreated.

A small colored boy, about nine years old, was set upon at the corner of Broadway and Chambers Street by the mob. He jumped on a two-horse wagon that was passing by, when sticks and stones were hurled at him from every quarter. We believe the poor little fellow escaped.

The Orphan Asylum (in Fifth Avenue, near Forty-sixth Street), was fired about five o'clock in the afternoon. The infuriated mob, eager for any outrage, were turned that way by the simple suggestion that the building was full of colored children. They clamored around the house like demons, filling the air with yells. A few policemen, who attempted to make a stand, were instantly overpowered—several being severely or fatally injured. While this was going on, a few of the less evil disposed gave notice to the inmates to quit the building.

The sight of the helpless creatures stayed, for a moment, even the insensate mob; but the orphans were no sooner out than the work of demolition commenced. First the main building was gutted and then set on fire. While it was burning, the large wing adjoining—used as a dormitory—was stripped, inside and out. . . .

On the Philippines (1898)*

Finley Peter Dunne

Finley Peter Dunne (1867–1936) was a Chicago journalist who created the immortal commentator on the news, Mr. Dooley. Martin Dooley (dates unknown) was an Irish bartender who, with wry wit, educated his daily customer, Mr. Hennessy, who had, in Dunne's words, "at best but a clouded view of public affairs." In this selection Mr. Hennessy was speaking for President William McKinley (Mack) who decided to annex the Philippines although, in fact, he had not known where they were located a few months before. Dunne effectively satirized the ignorance with which most of the nation embraced imperialism.

"I know what I'd do if I was Mack," said Mr. Hennessy. "I'd hist a flag over th' Ph'lippeens, an' I'd take in th' whole lot iv thim."

---

* From Finley Peter Dunne, *Mr. Dooley in Peace and War* (New York: Small, Maynard & Co., 1901), pp. 43–47.

"An' yet," said Mr. Dooley, "'tis not more thin two months since ye larned whether they were islands or canned goods. Yer back yard is so small that yer cow can't turn r-round without buttin' th' woodshed off th' premises, an' ye wudden't go out to th' stock yards without takin' out a policy on yer life. Suppose ye was standin' at th' corner iv State Sthreet an' Archey R-road, wud ye know what car to take to get to th' Ph'lippeens? If yer son Packy was to ask ye where th' Ph'lippeens is, cud ye give him anny good idea whether they was in Rooshia or jus' west iv th' thracks?"

"Mebbe I cudden't," said Mr. Hennessy, haughtily, "but I'm f'r takin' thim in, annyhow."

"So might I be," said Mr. Dooley, "if I cud on'y get me mind on it. Wan iv the worst things about this here war is th' way it's makin' puzzles f'r our poor, tired heads. Whin I wint into it, I thought all I'd have to do was to set up here behind th' bar with a good tin-cint see-gar in me teeth, an' toos dinnymite bombs into th' hated city iv Havana. But look at me now. Th' war is still goin' on; an' ivry night, whin I'm countin' up the cash, I'm askin' mesilf will I annex Cubia or lave it to the Cubians? Will I take Porther Ricky [Puerto Rico] or put it by? An' what shud I do with the Ph'lippeens? Oh, what shud I do with thim? I can't annex thim because I don't know where they ar-re. I can't let go iv thim because some wan else'll take thim if I do. They are eight thousan' iv them islands, with a popylation iv wan hundherd millyon naked savages; an' me bedroom's crowded now with me an' th' bed. How can I take thim in, an' how on earth am I goin' to cover th' nakedness iv thim savages with me wan shoot iv clothes? An' yet 'twud break me heart to think iv givin' people I niver see or heerd tell iv back to other people I don't know. An', if I don't take thim, Schwartzmeister down th' sthreet, that has half me thrade already, will grab thim sure.

"It ain't that I'm afraid iv not doin' th' r-right thing in th' end, Hinnissy. Some mornin' I'll wake up an' know jus' what to do, an' that I'll do. But 'tis th' annoyance in th' mane time. I've been r-readin' about th' counthry. 'Tis over beyant yer left shoulder whin ye're facin' east. Jus' throw yer thumb back, an' ye have it as ac'rate as anny man in town. 'Tis farther thin Boohlgahrya an' not so far as Blewchoochoo. It's near Chiny, an' it's not so near; an', if a man was to bore a well through fr'm Goshen, Indianny, he might sthrike it, an' thin again he might not. It's a poverty-sthricken counthry, full iv goold an' precious stones, where th' people can pick dinner off th' threes an' ar-re starvin' because they have no stepladders. Th' inhabitants is mostly naygurs an' Chinnymen, peaceful, industhrus, an' lawabidin', but savage an' bloodthirsty in their methods. They wear no clothes except what they have on, an' each woman has five husbands an' each man has five wives. Th' r-rest goes into th' discard, th' same as here. Th' islands has been ownded be Spain since befure th' fire; an' she's threated thim so well they're now up in ar-rms again her, except a majority iv thim which is thurly loyal. Th' natives seldom fight, but whin they get made at wan another they r-run-a-muck. Whin a man r-runs-a-muck sometimes they hang him an' sometimes they discharge him an' hire a new motorman. Th' women ar-re beautiful, with languishin' black eyes, an' they smoke see-gars, but ar-re hurried an' incomplete in their dhress. I see a pitcher iv wan th' other day with nawthin' on her but a basket of cocoanuts an' a hoop-skirt. They're no prudes. We import juke, hemp, cigar wrappers, sugar, an' fairy tales fr'm th' Ph'lippeens, an' export six-inch shells an' th' like. Iv late th' Ph'lippeens has awaked to th' fact that they're behind th' times, an' has received much American amminition in their midst. They say th' Spanyards is all tore up about it.

"I larned all this fr'm th' papers, an' I know 'tis sthraight. An' yet, Hinnissy, I dinnaw what to do about th' Ph'lippeens. An' I'm all alone in th' wurruld. Ivrybody else has made up his mind. Ye ask anny con-ducthor on Ar-rchy R-road, an' he'll tell ye. Ye can find out fr'm the papers; an', if ye really want to know, all ye have to do is to ask a prom'nent citizen who can mow all th' lawn he owns with a safety razor. But I don't know."

"Hang on to thim," said Mr. Hennessy, stoutly. "What we've got we must hold."

"Well," said Mr. Dooley, "if I was Mack, I'd lave it to George.* I'd say: 'George,' I'd say, 'if ye're f'r hangin' on, hang on it is. If ye say, lave go, I dhrop thim.' 'Twas George won thim with th' shells, an' th' question's up to him."

---

* It was Commodore George Dewey (soon Admiral) who had easily taken Manila Bay on May 1, 1898.

The Socialist Party against War and Militarism (1917)*

When war broke out in Europe in 1914, German, French, and British socialists immediately reneged on their oft-repeated pledges not to participate in any inter-national war but instead to take the opportunity of war to make a revolution. Only the Italian socialists and the underground movement in Czarist Russia clung to their principles. Although this abandonment of first principle was a serious blow to American socialists, the American Socialist Party did not follow the European example when the United States entered the war in April, 1917.

Meeting in emergency convention in St. Louis, party delegates adopted a ringing denunciation of the war which was later ratified by the membership. Many of the party's prominent leaders broke with the party on the question and rallied behind the war effort. But the rank-and-file was largely untouched and, in fact, the party grew during the war, indicating that anti-war sentiment did not die with America's declaration. The party suffered many harassments during the war but emerged to win more votes than ever in the presidential election of 1920. It faded from the political scene during the twenties for reasons unrelated to its wartime opposition. These majority "Resolutions on War and Militarism" (there were two alternate plans) were written by Morris Hillquit, one of the leaders of the party in New York City.

The Socialist Party of the United States in the present grave crisis solemnly reaffirms its allegiance to the principle of internationalism and working class solidarity the world over, and proclaims its un-alterable opposition to the war just declared by the government of the United States.

Modern wars as a rule have been caused by the commercial and financial rivalry and intrigues of the capitalist interests in the different countries. Whether they have been frankly waged as wars of aggression or have been hypocritically represented as wars of defense, they have always been made by the classes and fought by the masses. Wars bring wealth and power to the ruling classes, and suffering, death and demoralization to the workers.

They breed a sinister spirit of passion, unreason, race hatred, and false patriotism. They obscure the struggles of the workers for life, liberty and social justice. They tend to sever the vital bonds of solidarity between them and their brothers in other countries, to destroy their organizations and to curtail their civic and political rights and liberties.

The Socialist Party of the United States is unalterably opposed to the system of exploitation and class rule which is upheld and strength-

* From Nathan Fine, *Labor and Farmer Parties in the United States* (New York: The Rand School, 1928), pp. 310–14.

ened by military power and sham national patriotism. We therefore call upon the workers of all countries to refuse support to their governments in their wars. The wars of the contending national groups of capitalists are not the concern of the workers. The only struggle which would justify the workers in taking up arms is the great struggle of the working class of the world to free itself from economic exploitation and political oppression, and we particularly warn the workers against the snare and delusion of defensive warfare. As against the false doctrine of national patriotism we uphold the ideal of international working-class solidarity. In support of capitalism, we will not willingly give a single life or a single dollar; in support of the struggle of the workers for freedom we pledge our all.

The mad orgy of death and destruction which is now convulsing unfortunate Europe was caused by the conflict of capitalist interests in the European countries.

In each of these countries the workers were oppressed and exploited. They produced enormous wealth but the bulk of it was withheld from them by the owners of the industries. The workers were thus deprived of the means to repurchase the wealth which they themselves had created.

The capitalist class of each country was forced to look for foreign markets to dispose of the accumulated "surplus" wealth. The huge profits made by the capitalists could no longer be profitably reinvested in their own countries, hence, they were driven to look for foreign fields of investment. The geographical boundaries of each modern capitalist country thus became too narrow for the industrial and commercial operations of its capitalist class.

The efforts of the capitalists of all leading nations were therefore centered upon the domination of the world markets. Imperialism became the dominant note in the politics of Europe. The acquisition of colonial possessions and the extension of spheres of commercial and political influence became the object of diplomatic intrigues and the cause of constant clashes between nations.

The acute competition between the capitalist powers of the earth, their jealousies and distrusts of one another, and the fear of the rising power of the working class forced each of them to arm to the teeth. This led to the mad rivalry of armament, which, years before the outbreak of the present war had turned the leading countries of Europe into armed camps with standing armies of many millions, drilled and equipped for war in times of "peace."

Capitalism, imperialism and militarism had thus laid the foundation of an inevitable general conflict in Europe. The ghastly war in Europe was not caused by an accidental event, nor by the policy or institutions of any single nation. It was the logical outcome of the competitive capitalist system.

The six million men of all countries and races who have been ruthlessly slain in the first thirty months of this war, the millions of others who have been crippled and maimed, the vast treasures of ruthlessly slain in the first thirty months of this war, the millions of others who have been crippled and maimed, the vast treasures of wealth that have been destroyed, the untold misery and sufferings of Europe, have not been sacrifices exacted in a struggle for principles or ideals, but wanton offerings upon the altar of private profit.

The forces of capitalism which have led to the war in Europe are even more hideously transparent in the war recently provoked by the ruling class of this country.

When Belgium was invaded, the government enjoined upon the people of this country the duty of remaining neutral, thus clearly demonstrating that the "dictates of humanity" and the fate of small nations and of democratic institutions were matters that did not concern it. But when our enormous war traffic was seriously threatened, our government called upon us to rally to the "defense of democracy and civilization."

Our entrance into the European war was instigated by the predatory capitalists in the United States who boast of the enormous profit of seven billion dollars from the manufacture and sale of munitions and war supplies and from the exportation of American food stuffs and other necessaries. They are also deeply interested in the continuance of war and the success of the allied arms through their huge loans to the governments of the allied powers and through other commercial ties. It is the same interests which strive for imperialistic domination of the Western Hemisphere.

The war of the United States against Germany cannot be justified even on the plea that it is a war in defense of American rights or American "honor." Ruthless as the unrestricted submarine war policy of the German government was and is, it is not an invasion of the rights of American people as such, but only an interference with the opportunity of certain groups of American capitalists to coin cold profits out of the blood and sufferings of our fellow men in the warring countries of Eurpoe.

It is not a war against the militarist regime of the Central Powers. Militarism can never be abolished by militarism.

It is not a war to advance the cause of democracy in Europe. Democracy can never be imposed upon any country by a foreign power by force of arms.

It is a cant and hypocrisy to say that the war is not directed against the German people, but against the Imperial government of Germany. If we send an armed force to the battlefields of Europe, its cannon will mow down the masses of the German people and not the Imperial German government.

Our entrance into the European conflict at this time will serve only to multiply the horrors of the war, to increase the toll of death and destruction and to prolong the fiendish slaughter. It will bring death, suffering and destitution to the people of the United States and particularly to the working class. It will give the powers of reaction in this country the pretext for an attempt to throttle our rights and to crush our democratic institutions, and to fasten upon this country a permanent militarism.

The working class of the United States has no quarrel with the working class of Germany or of any other country. The people of the United States have no quarrel with the people of Germany or of any other country. The American people did not want and do not want this war. They have not been consulted about the war and have had no part in declaring war. They have been plunged into this war by the trickery and treachery of the ruling class of the country through its representatives in the national Administration and national Congress, its demogogic agitators, its subsidized press, and other servile instruments of public expression.

We brand the declaration of war by our government as a crime against the people of the United States and against the nations of the world.

In all modern history there has been no war more unjustifiable than the war in which we are about to engage.

No greater dishonor has ever been forced upon a people than that which the capitalist class is forcing upon this nation against its will.

In harmony with these principles, the Socialist Party emphatically rejects the proposal that in time of war the workers should suspend their struggle for better conditions. On the contrary, the acute situation created by war calls for an even more vigorous prosecution of the class struggle, and we recommend to the workers and pledge ourselves to the following course of action:

1) Continuous, active, and public opposition to the war, through demonstrations, mass petitions, and all other means within our power.

2) Unyielding opposition to all proposed legislations for military or industrial conscription. Should such conscription be forced upon the people, we pledge ourselves to continuous efforts for the repeal of such laws and to the support of all mass movements in opposition to conscription. We pledge ourselves to oppose with all our strength any attempt to raise money for payment of war expense by taxing the necessaries of life or issuing bonds which will put the burden upon future generations. We demand that the capitalist class, which is responsible for the war, pay its cost. Let those who kindled the fire, furnish the fuel.

3) Vigorous resistance to all reactionary measures such as censorship of press and mails, restriction of the rights of free speech, assemblage, and organization, or compulsory arbitration and limitation of the right to strike.

4) Consistent propaganda against military training and militaristic teaching in the public schools.

5) Extension of the campaign of education among the workers to organize them into strong, class-conscious, and closely unified political and industrial organizations, to enable them by concerted and harmonious mass action to shorten this war and to establish lasting peace.

6) Widespread educational propaganda to enlighten the masses as to the true relation between capitalism and war, and to rouse and organize them for action, not only against present war evils, but for the prevention of future wars and for the destruction of the causes of war.

7) To protect the masses of the American people from the pressing danger of starvation which the war in Europe has brought upon them, and which the entry of the United States has already accentuated, we demand:

(a) The restriction of food exports so long as the present shortage continues, the fixing of maximum prices, and whatever measures may be necessary to prevent the food speculators from holding back the supplies now in their hands;

(b) The socialization and democratic management of the great industries concerned with the production, transportation, storage, and the marketing of food and other necessaries of life;

(c) The socialization and democratic management of all land and other natural resources now held out of use for monopolistic or speculative profit.

These measures are presented as means of protecting the workers against the evil results of the present war. The danger of recurrence of war will exist as long as the capitalist system of industry remains in existence. The end of wars will come with the establishment of socialized industry and industrial democracy the world over. The Socialist Party calls upon all the workers to join it in its struggle to reach this goal, and thus bring into the world a new society in which peace, fraternity, and human brotherhood will be the dominant ideals.

Recommendations

1) We recommend that the convention instruct our elected representatives in Congress, in the state legislatures, and in local bodies, to vote against all proposed appropriations or loans for military, naval, and other war purposes.

2) We recommend that this convention instruct the National Executive Committee to extend and improve the propaganda among women, because they as housewives and as mothers are now particularly ready to accept our message.

3) We recommend that the convention instruct the National Executive Committee to initiate an organized movement of Socialists, organized workers, and other anti-war forces for concerted action along the lines of this program.

(Signed)

KATE RICHARDS O'HARE, *Chairman*	FRANK MIDNEY
VICTOR L. BERGER	PATRICK QUINLAN
JOB HARRIMAN	C. E. RUTHENBERG
MORRIS HILLQUIT	MAYNARD SHIPLEY
DAN HOGAN	GEORGE SPIESS, JR.
	ALGERNON LEE, *Secretary*

This Unholy War (1917)*

George Norris

While socialists emphasized the imperialistic nature of the war, Progressives like Senator George Norris of Nebraska (1861–1944) were interested only secondarily in the nature of the European conflict and determined only that the United States stay out. They saw the movement toward involvement in the war as calculated to benefit munitions makers and bankers who had a stake in an allied victory. Norris and his associates, like Senator Robert M. La Follette of Wisconsin, said that the Administration was an active accomplice in this movement to embroil the United States. In his speech before the Senate on April 4, 1917, Norris traced American partisanship in the conflict while the nation was still ostensibly neutral.

The resolution now before the Senate is a declaration of war. Before taking this momentous step, and while standing on the brink of this terrible vortex, we ought to pause and calmly and judiciously consider the terrible consequences of the step we are about to take. We ought to consider likewise the route we have recently traveled and ascertain whether we have reached our present position in a way that is compatible with the neutral position which we claimed to occupy at the beginning and through the various stages of this unholy and unrighteous war.

No close student of recent history will deny that both Great Britain and Germany have, on numerous occasions since the beginning of the war, flagrantly violated in the most serious manner the rights of neutral vessels and neutral nations under existing international law as recognized up to the beginning of this war by the civilized world.

The reason given by the President in asking Congress to declare war against Germany is that the German government has declared certain war zones, within which, by the use of submarines, she sinks, without notice, American ships and destroys American lives.

Let us trace briefly the origin and history of these so-called war zones. The first war zone was declared by Great Britain. She gave us and the world notice of it on the 4th day of November, 1914. The zone became effective November 5, 1914, the next day after the notice was given. This zone so declared by Great Britain covered the whole of the North Sea. The order establishing it sought to close the north of Scotland route around the British Isles to Denmark, Holland,

---

* From the *Congressional Record*, 65th Congress, Sess. I, pp. 212–214.

Norway, Sweden, and the Baltic Sea. The decree of establishment drew an arbitrary line from the Hebrides Islands along the Scottish coast to Iceland, and warned neutral shipping that it would cross those lines at its peril, and ordered that ships might go to Holland and other neutral nations by taking the English Channel route through the Straight of Dover.

The first German war zone was declared on the 4th day of February, 1915, just three months after the British war zone was declared. Germany gave fifteen days' notice of the establishment of her zone, which became effective on the 18th day of February, 1915. The German war zone covered the English Channel and the high sea waters around the British Isles. It sought to close the English Channel route around the British Isles to Holland, Norway, Sweden, Denmark, and the Baltic Sea. The German war zone decreed that neutral vessels would be exposed to danger in the English Channel route, but that the route around the north of Scotland and in the eastern part of the North Sea, in a strip thirty miles wide along the Dutch coast, would be free from danger.

It will thus be seen that the British government declared the north of Scotland route into the Baltic Sea as dangerous and the English Channel route into the Baltic Sea as safe.

The German government in its order did exactly the reverse. It declared the north of Scotland route into the Baltic Sea as safe and the English Channel route into the Baltic Sea as dangerous.

The order of the British government declaring the North Sea as a war zone used the following language:

> The British Admiralty gives notice that the waters of the North Sea must be considered a military area. Within this area merchant shipping of all kinds, traders of all countries, fishing craft, and other vessels will be exposed to the gravest danger from mines it has been necessary to lay.

The German government, by its order declaring its war zone around the south of England, declared that the order would be made effective by the use of submarines.

Thus we have the two declarations of the two governments, each declaring a military zone and warning neutral shipping from going into the prohibited area. England sought to make her order effective by the use of submerged mines. Germany sought to make her order effective by the use of submarines. Both of these orders were illegal and contrary to all international law as well as the principles of humanity. Under international law no belligerent government has the right to place submerged mines in the high seas. Neither has it any right to take human life without notice by the use of submarines. If there is any difference on the ground of humanity between these two instrumentalities, it is certainly in favor of the submarines. The submarine can exercise some degree of discretion and judgment. The submerged mine always destroys without notice, friend and foe alike, guilty and innocent the same. In carrying out these two policies, both Great Britain and Germany have sunk American ships and destroyed American lives without provocation and without notice. There have been more ships sunk and more American lives lost from the action of submarines than from English mines in the North Sea; for the simple reason that we finally acquiesced in the British war zone and kept our ships out of it, while in the German war zone we have refused to recognize its legality and have not kept either our ships or our citizens out of its area. If American ships had gone into the British war zone in defiance of Great Britain's order, as they have gone into the German war zone in defiance of the German government's order, there would have been many more American lives lost and many more American ships sunk by the instrumentality of the mines than the instrumentality of the submarines.

We have in the main complied with the demands made by Great Britain. Our ships have followed the instructions of the British government in going not only to England but to the neutral nations of the world, and in thus complying with the British order American ships going to Holland, Denmark, Norway, and Sweden have been taken by British officials into British ports and their cargoes inspected and examined. All the mails we have carried even to neutral countries have been opened and censored, and oftentimes the entire cargo confiscated by the government. Nothing has been permitted to pass to even the most neutral nations except after examination and with the permission of the officials of the British government.

.   .   .   .

There are a great many American citizens who feel that we owe it as a duty to humanity to take part in this war. Many instances of cruelty and inhumanity can be found on both sides. Men are often biased in their judgment on account of their sympathy and their interests. To my mind, what we ought to have maintained from the beginning was the strictest neutrality. If we had done this I do not believe we would have been on the verge of war at the present time. We had a right as a nation, if we desired, to cease at any time to be neutral. We had a technical right to respect the English war zone and to disregard the German war zone, but we could not do that and be neutral. I have no quarrel to find with the man who does not desire our country to remain neutral. While many such people are moved by selfish motives and hopes of gain, I have no doubt but that in a great many instances, through what I believe to be a misunderstanding of the real condition, there are many honest, patriotic citizens who think we ought to engage in this war and who are behind the President in his demand that we should declare war against Germany. I think such people err in judgment and to a great extent have been misled as to the real history and the true facts by the almost unanimous demand of the great combination of wealth that has a direct financial interest in our participation in the war. We have loaned many hundreds of millions of dollars to the allies in this controversy. While such action was legal and countenanced by international law, there is no doubt in my mind but the enormous amount of money loaned to the allies in this country has been instrumental in bringing about a public sentiment in favor of our country taking a course that would make every bond worth a hundred cents on the dollar and making the payment of every debt certain and sure. Through this instrumentality and also through the instrumentality of others who have not only made millions out of the war in the manufacture of munitions, etc., and who would expect to make millions more if our country can be drawn into the catastrophe, a large number of the great newspapers and news agencies of the country have been controlled and enlisted in the greatest propaganda that the world has ever known, to manufacture sentiment in favor of war. It is now demanded that the American citizens shall be used as insurance policies to guarantee the safe delivery of munitions of war to belligerent nations. The enormous profits of munition manufacturers, stockbrokers, and bond dealers must be still further increased by our entrance into the war.

.   .   .   .

We are going into war upon the command of gold. We are going to run the risk of sacrificing millions of our countrymen's lives in order that other countrymen may coin their lifeblood into money. And even if we do not cross the Atlantic and go into the trenches, we are going to pile up a debt that the toiling masses that shall come many generations after us will have to pay. Unborn millions will bend their backs in toil in order to pay for the terrible step we are now about to take. We are about to do the bidding of wealth's terrible mandate. By our act we will make millions of our countrymen suffer, and the consequences of it may well be that millions of our brethren must shed their lifeblood, millions of broken-hearted women must weep, millions of children must suffer with cold, and millions of babes must die from hunger, and all because we want to preserve the commercial right of American citizens to deliver munitions of war to belligerent nations.

.   .   .   .

I know that I am powerless to stop it. I know that this war madness has taken possession of the financial and political powers of our country. I know that nothing I can say will stay the blow that is soon to fall. I feel that we are committing a sin against humanity and against our countrymen. I would like to say to this war god, "You shall not coin into gold the lifeblood of my brethren." I would like to prevent this terrible catastrophe from falling upon my people. I would be willing to surrender my own life if I could cause this awful cup to pass. I charge no man here with a wrong motive, but it seems to me that this war craze has robbed us of our judgment. I wish we might delay our action until reason could again be enthroned in the brain of man. I feel that we are about to put the dollar sign upon the American flag.

Christians at War*

John Kendrick (IWW)

The Wobblies were the worst persecuted of the anti-war organizations in the United States. Offices of the revolutionary union were raided and, in one trial alone, a hundred leaders of the union were sentenced to prison for interfering with the war effort.

Ironically, the IWW was by no means the most active opponent of the war. It was opposed to the war, but the union was fatalistic on the question, realizing that it was too weak to do anything about American entrance and hoping only to ride the conflict out. The Wobblies even attempted to accommodate to the wartime hysteria. Anti-war songs such as "Christians at War," a parody of "Onward Christian Soldiers," were deleted from wartime editions of the Little Red Songbook, a collection of revolutionary IWW songs. The union is virtually gone now, but has left a biting legacy in songs like "Christians at War."

_____

* This song has appeared in numerous editions of *Songs of the Workers to Fan the Flames of Discontent* (Chicago: Industrial Workers of the World). It is reprinted here by permission.

Onward, Christian soldiers! Duty's way is plain;
Slay your Christian neighbors, or by them be slain.
Pulpiteers are spouting effervescent will,
God above is calling you to rob and rape and kill,
All your acts are sanctified by the Lamb on high;
If you love the Holy Ghost, go murder, pray and die.

Onward, Christian soldiers, rip and tear and smite!
Let the gentle Jesus bless your dynamite.
Splinter skulls with shrapnel, fertilize the sod;
Folks who do not speak your tongue deserve the curse of God.
Smash the doors of every home, pretty maidens seize;
Use your might and sacred right to treat them as you please.

Onward, Christian soldiers! Eat and drink your fill;
Rob with bloody fingers, Christ okays the bill.
Steal the farmers' savings, take their grain and meat;
Even though the children starve, the Saviour's bums must eat.
Burn the peasants' cottages, orphans leave bereft;
In Jehovah's holy name, wreak ruin right and left.

Onward, Christian soldiers! Drench the land with gore;
Mercy is a weakness all the gods abhor.
Bayonet the babies; jab the mothers too;
Hoist the cross of Calvary to hallow all you do.
File your bullets' noses flat, poison every well;
God decrees your enemies must all go plumb to hell.

Onward, Christian soldiers, blighting all you meet,
Trampling human freedom under pious feet.
Praise the Lord whose dollar sign dupes his favorite race!
Make the foreign trash respect your bullion brand of grace.
Trust in mock salvation, serve as pirates' tools;
History will say of you: "That pack of G - - d - - - fools."

Assumptions about War (1941)

Stuart Chase

The America First Committee was founded in 1940 at the bleakest moment of the British war effort. German troops were poised on the English Channel and the invasion of England appeared imminent. The America Firsters, including such luminaries as Charles Lindbergh and Chester Bowles, argued that the United States should avoid the mistake of World War I and keep out of European quarrels. The Committee represented the last gasp of between-war American isolationism and also the conviction that the British cause in Europe was lost.

The America Firsters were accused of pro-Nazi inclinations. This was not true although they did not regard a German victory in Europe as fearful enough a portent to go to war to avoid it. The Committee urged a defensive armament at home so that Germany would not dare challenge the United States to a war.

The leaflet excerpted here, "Four Assumptions About the War" by Stuart Chase, was printed by the Chicago America First Committee in January, 1941. It sums up the Committee's point of view at a time when perhaps 80 per cent of the nation's people did not want involvement in the war.

Our relative stability is compounded of many factors—our continental size, our natural resources, our geographical isolation, our dominating position in the hemisphere, our democratic habits practiced by generations of pioneer ancestors. As a result of these factors we have few wars in the hemisphere, fewer armed revolts, no fortified frontiers, and good neighbors north and south. Our standards of living are higher than anywhere else in the world today. This does not mean that living standards are adequate for all classes of people; only that they are unchallenged elsewhere and are, in most areas, well above the line of starvation, despair and revolt.

In the United States, citizens elect their leaders and have wide latitudes in the exercise of free speech, free press, free assembly, free worship, and freedom from being pushed around by autocrats, land owners, gentlemen in colored shirts, and the secret police. They are not immune from being pushed around—witness the Negroes and the Okies—but relative to Old World citizens, they are free men. Even in Britain, Sweden, Switzerland today, one has to do what the authorities tell one to do, or else.

A major test of stability was the Great Depression of 1929, which presently caused Europe to fall apart, but only rocked without shattering the Americas. We have found a sound culture bed. From this base, rough as it is, great developments are clearly visible—the abolition of poverty, unprecedented improvements in health and energy, a towering renaissance in the arts; an architecture and an engineering to challenge the gods. Towards these ends we are groping, with firm ground under our feet. We are the New World. We are the hope of mankind. Our culture is not burdened with the terrible dead weights which the Old World must carry.

Countries in the Old World do not have this stability. Just because they are old they are vulnerable to the impact of high technology. Their instability hardly needs documentation. Look at any edition of any newspaper: Britain fighting heroically for her life, as customs centuries old are melted down beneath the bombs. The British Empire swaying on the brink. The obliteration of France in a shadow so black we almost forget it is there at all. The frozen communities of Belgium, Holland, Scandinavia, Switzerland. The murderous tension in the Balkans, with boundary lines snapping in all directions. The gutted shell of Spain. The Mediterranean as the new Dead Sea. The gory deadlock in China. Terror in Iran, Africa and the East Indies. A precarious stability depending on one man's will in Germany, Russia, Italy.

Even in the best of times, Old World communities carry a load of unstable elements, largely lacking in the Americas. Consider the fractures implicit on a continent with twenty-five or more languages, tariff walls and currencies; with inadequate natural resources, with class divisions, violent ideologies, violent politics, bloody historical feuds. These cleavages were bad enough in the handicraft age. In the power age they make the culture unworkable. How many years, decades, will it take to steam-roller these differences into a stable pattern which can guarantee both goods and freedom? Power age communities need to be continental in scope to fit an expanding technology. Hitler now announces a new order in Europe. God knows Europe needs it, but one wonders if Hitler can do more than set up a kind of vineyard on Vesuvius. It looks as if the choice in Europe was to give up either nationalism or technology. Crusades to restore the rights of small nations will crash into the technological imperative, and vice versa. Can anyone resolve this crazy quilt but the people of Europe themselves? The British have not even suggested what they propose to do about it if they win.

The United States cannot solve the political and economic problems of Europe, Asia, Africa, and the Indies by armed assault on their totalitarian leaders. Consider what is involved. First, a military adventure—and we cannot possibly equip ourselves for military adventures overseas before 1944 at the earliest—in which America takes on Germany, Italy, and Japan with their smaller allies, and before the show is over perhaps Russia, Spain, and France as well. Britain might be more of a liability than an asset in this adventure because of the extreme vulnerability of the British Isles. Pledged to defend this outpost, now flanked by enemy bases and ringed on the west by fleets of submarines, we should be severely handicapped in our efforts to make a frontal assault on the European, African, or Asiatic mainland. If we confined our military effort solely to the defense of Britain, we might save the British Isles, and we might not. It would, I suspect, be a full-time job, and leave us little energy for the reduction of Berlin, Rome, Tokyo, Madrid, and Moscow.

On the fantastic assumption that all these capitals were in our hands, what then? Our work would have just begun. Then we should have to find a social framework to fit some 1.5 billion people, burdened with the cleavages just mentioned, and say to them: "Take this and like it." We can be quite sure that many of them, perhaps most of them, won't like it. So then we might try to make them like it. One way would be to keep a few million American boys, armed to the teeth, in constant attendance to see that they like it. Another would be concentration camps. Another would be puppet governments with strings pulled from Washington.

How long would this educational program take? How long should we be in establishing our new order in Europe, Asia, Africa and the Indies? And what if the blueprint turned out to be no good? Would the pattern we impose fit the revolutionary changes that are already far gone in those parts? Whom, by the way, would you nominate to prepare the blueprints—Mr. Walter Lippmann, Mr. Jesse Jones, Mr. Hoover? When people say we ought to go and help Britain knock out Hitler and restore democracy, the free market, and the little nations, they apparently have no conception of what such a crusade entails. Their imaginations go riotously to the shooting of Hitler, and there they stop. I grant it is a satisfying picture, but unfortunately the removal of Hitler would be only a preliminary incident in the total task before us.

Americans are fine, upstanding, enterprising folks. They could probably organize and defend the whole Western Hemisphere by giving their entire attention to the job. Or they might possibly win a stalemate peace for Britain which would preserve her shattered island and her honor. But I do not see how they can do what I have indicated above. Giving Britain her island and her honor, furthermore, settles nothing, with Europe and Asia still in totalitarian hands.

If Americans attempt this program, whether they knock out the dictators or not, they will most assuredly wreck their own New World pattern. As I said, we are an enterprising people. When we start a thing we like to finish it. We have never lost a war yet. With war once declared, or acts of war committed, there would be no end except victory or defeat—unless it were the utter exhaustion of both sides.

The consequences to our culture of an all-out war abroad are simply told— . . . the liquidation of political democracy, of Congress, the Supreme Court, private enterprise, the banks, free press and free speech; the persecution of German-Americans and Italian-Americans, witch hunts, forced labor, fixed prices, rationing, astronomical debts, and the rest. We would become as a people tough, cruel and vindictive. Scientific research would go to pot. With the whole world on our hands, draining our life blood overseas, we would have no time and no desire to plan for the America of the future. Our pattern would be smashed beyond repair.

Korea (1952)

Dwight D. Eisenhower

The question of peace during the Korean War had a bizarre career. On the one hand, there was less of movement opposed to that war than to any other American war. The apparent baldness of North Korea's aggression against the South precluded any great sympathy for America's enemy outside the emasculated and minescule Communist organizations. Even staunch internationalists rallied behind the war effort because, formally, the United States was acting for the United Nations. There was, in short, no anti-war movement in the usual sense of the term; most Americans accepted the government's assumption that "communism" must be stopped.

At the same time, however, Americans grew war-weary during the conflict as they never had since the Civil War. The North Korean and Chinese troops fought the United States to a stalemate, an unpleasant fact to Americans bred in the erroneous "never-a-lost-war" tradition. The only alternative to a compromise settlement—along the lines of the *status quo ante bellum*—was a war with China which most military leaders believed would be disastrous. Americans hated communism, to be sure, but they also wanted relief from the war.

The strategists of General Dwight D. Eisenhower's campaign for the presidency grasped this anomaly and formulated a policy which won the election. The war was the avoidable blunder of a corrupt administration, they argued. Had the United States made its power and intentions known, the attack would never have occurred. A good anti-communist foreign policy would be to wage Cold War with such pressure that communists would fear to start "hot" wars.

In the meantime, the Korean affair had been so badly botched that the only alternative was to settle it quickly and "honorably." Only a new administration could do this; the old party was too deeply committed to its bankrupt policy to effect a change.

By the end of his campaign, Eisenhower emphasized this issue virtually to the exclusion of the "mess in Washington" theme which had characterized its early stages. He won overwhelmingly.

These are exerpts from three speeches in which he stated the policy.

San Francisco, October 8, 1952:

Without weakening the security of the free world I pledge full dedication to the job of finding an intelligent and honorable way to end the tragic toll of American casualties in Korea. For this war is reaching tonight into the homes of thousands of American families.

I do not believe that Korea must forever be a part of our American daily life. The South Korean Ambassador has recently said:

"Give us guns; spare your sons."

Here one way is pointed. I shall never say as the present Administration says: "Because the problem is tough the problem can't be solved."

Today the world dwells in a twilight zone between peace and war—a zone we call "Cold War." What courses of action lie before us in shaping national policy?

One is to appease. That is a proven folly.

A second course would be to adopt a stupidly agressive attitude and so markedly increase the risk of global war. Modern war is not a conceivable choice in framing national policy. War would do unthinkable damage to every moral and material value we cherish.

War is the last desperate resort when freedom itself is at stake.

The third course is to prosecute the Cold War in which we now find ourselves with vigor and wisdom. . . . Remember this: we wage a Cold War in order to escape the horror of its opposite—war itself.

In Cold War we do not use an arsenal of arms and armaments. Rather, we use all means short of war to lead men to believe in the values that will preserve peace and freedom. Our aim in Cold War is not conquest of territory or subjugation by force. Our aim is more subtle, more pervasive, more complete.

Philadelphia, September 4, 1952:

Our initiative, imagination, and productive system are once more tied and shackled to the war and the prospect of war. Our economy is a war economy. Our prosperity is a war prosperity. And the awful fact of war reaches into every American family.

That is the record. Now the party that wrote that record asks us to underwrite it with a new lease of power. Is that the answer?

You and I know better.

If today the driver of a school bus in your town runs into a truck, and if tomorrow he hits a lamp post, and if the next day he drives into a ditch, what do you do? You don't say, "I like the bus driver; his intentions are good. I will risk the lives of our children." You don't say that. You get a new bus driver.

The people of America do not want war. . . . But whom can we trust for such a program? Whom can we trust to win the peace? The record in Korea will help find an answer to that question.

Detroit, October 24, 1952:

The biggest fact about the Korean War is this: it was never inevitable, it was never inescapable, no fantastic fiat of history decreed that little South Korea—in the summer of 1950—would fatally tempt Communist aggressors as their easiest victim. No demonic destiny decreed that America had to be bled this way in order to keep South Korea free and to keep freedom itself self-respecting.

We are not mere prisoners of history. That is a doctrine for totalitarians, it is no creed for free men.

There is a Korean War—and we are fighting it—for the simplest of reasons: because free leadership failed to check and to turn back Communist ambition before it savagely attacked us. The Korean War —more perhaps than any other war in history—simply and swiftly followed the collapse of our political defenses. There is no other reason than this: we failed to read and to outwit the totalitarian mind.

The Dominican Republic as Lyndon Johnson's Hungary (1965)

I. F. Stone

If the world survives the conflagration which I. F. Stone fears and wields his pen to avoid, he will probably be remembered as the greatest journalist of his era. After working as a staff writer for various liberal journals during the 1940's, Stone

founded his own publication, *I. F. Stone's Weekly* in 1952. It is a four-page newsletter, read widely by congressmen who rarely act on Stone's advice. The *Weekly*
looks skeptically at American policies and dissects American (and other nations') actions with an insight that rarely leaves Stone's targets standing firmly.

This article, from *I. F. Stone's Weekly* for May 31, 1965, attacks the double
standard which the United States government applies to its and Soviet Russia's
foreign policies.

The parallels between U.S. action in the Dominican Republic and
the Soviet Union's in Hungary are obvious. Our Monroe Doctrine is
like the Russian insistence on "friendly neighbors." The existence of
fringe elements—Fascist in Hungary, Communist in the Dominican
Republic—were used to smear both revolutions as extremist, though
both were motivated by a desire for democratization. Nagy's appeal
to the UN, like that of the Bosch forces, was opposed on the excuse
that the matter should be handled by regional organizations: in one
case the Warsaw Pact, in the other the OAS, each securely dominated
by its respective masters, Russian or American. Both great powers explained their conduct in the same way: the U.S.S.R. by fear of a Western
base, the U.S. by fear of a new Communist base, on its doorstep. In
both cases the presumed strategic need of the big power was the excuse
for riding roughshod over the wishes of the smaller neighbor, and in
neither were these exaggerated fears submitted to impartial scrutiny
by some international authority.

FBI Clearance for the Hemisphere

A less noticed parallel, now unfolding, is the naive and self-righteous
arrogance with which Washington and Moscow respectively took it on
themselves to decide just what kind of a government to allow their
small neighbor. Both great powers claimed to be avoiding "extremist"
solutions. Khrushchev and Mikoyan, themselves engaged in de-
Stalinizing the Soviet Union, did not want to put the Stalinists back
into power in Hungary. On the other hand, they did not want the
pendulum of freedom to swing so far that in their opinion it might
become "bourgeois," i.e. a regime of basic rights for the individual
instead of a milder variety of bureaucratic communism. They hauled
poor Kadar out of prison and once they had used him to crush the
revolution, they did slowly allow him to ease up the terror and permit
a little intellectual freedom on the edges. Similarly Johnson is busy
running the Dominican Republic by remote but unmistakable control:
a new government is being hand-picked from Washington. Its members
are even subjected to FBI clearance. We want, the All-Highest in the
White House says, neither a dictatorship of the right nor of the left.

It cannot be too authoritarian because that would embarrass us in our democratic pretensions. And it cannot be too democratic, because that might hurt U.S. investors.

This is the bitterest part of the spectacle for Latin Americans. Here we are beginning to play out again some of the most painful scenes of the Cuban and Mexican revolutions. When the Cubans, with belated and equivocal help from us, overthrew the Spanish yoke, the price they had to pay for getting rid of an American occupation was to allow foreign ownership of land: this intensified concentration of ownership of huge sugar holdings. It fastened on Cuba that mono-culture which impoverished its countryside and which Jose Marti and the revolutionaries were pledged to eradicate. In Mexico we waged a similar struggle against Article 27 of the revolutionary Constitution of 1917 which sought to recover mineral rights and peasant lands the dictator Diaz had given away to foreign, mostly American, interests. We withheld the recognition Mexico needed so badly for international credit reasons. Not until 1923, after private assurances that Article 27 would be interpreted laxly, did we recognize the Mexican Republic. Now we are doing something similar in the Dominican Republic. Though we claim to be waging a world-wide struggle for self-deter-mination and to allow diversity in the world (such is the language of our propaganda), the Dominican Constitution is being revised over long-distance telephone to suit Johnson's ideas.

L.B.J. As One-Man Constitutional Convention

Dan Kurzman of the *Washington Post* has the distinction of being the first American reporter to call attention to this development. The 1963 Constitution was the first ever to be framed and adopted by the Dominican people through wholly democratic processes. Mr. Justice Douglas was one of those who acted as consultant in its framing. It was to be a model for the hemisphere in establishing a secular state, with provisions for agrarian reform. In a dispatch published by his paper May 25, Kurzman disclosed that in the negotiations for a new government, pressure is being applied to revise the Constitution. One target is Article 19 which gives workers a right to profit-sharing in both industrial and agricultural enterprises. Another is Article 23 which prohibits large landholdings. A third is Article 25 which restricts the right of foreigners to acquire Dominican land. Another is Article 28, which requires landholders to sell that portion of their lands above the maximum fixed by law; the excess holdings would be resold to the landless peasantry. This is the agrarian reform we *say* we want in the hemisphere. It turns out that, as in Guatemala and in Cuba and in Mexico, we oppose it when it is enacted. An amendment is being proposed, Kurzman reports, to exempt owners of sugar plantations and cattle ranges. Central Romana, a subsidiary of the American-owned South Porto Rico Sugar Company, holds thousands of acres of the country's best sugar and cattle lands (see Selden Rodman's sympathetic history of the Dominican Republic, *Quisqueya*). Such are the conditions for American approval. And such is the reality behind our claim to be saving the hemisphere from Communism.

In the past half century at home, one basic social reform after another has been assailed as communistic by the masters of our big business enterprises; the Square Deal of Teddy Roosevelt, the New Freedom of Woodrow Wilson, the New Deal of Franklin D. Roosevelt all were opposed as undermining property and free enterprise. At home we have defeated these reactionary forces, though far from completely. But abroad they continue unchallenged to mold our policy. Our Latin American neighbors have been forced by military power, our own or local forces we armed, to bow to the will of Standard Oil and United Fruit and Anaconda Copper and Hanna Mining and any number of great North American enterprises. What they have been unable to block at home by invoking the Red Menace, they succeed in doing among our Latin neighbors. This is why the new Christian Democratic regime in Chile, fresh from a victory over a domestic Popular Front, is yet so deeply hostile to what we are doing in the Dominican Republic. This is why the OAS force we are trying to muster as our mercenaries is made up entirely (except for twenty policemen from Costa Rica) of forces supplied by the military dictatorships we helped install in Brazil, Honduras, and Nicaragua. The Johnson Doctrine aims by force to make Latin America safe for U.S. investment at whatever cost to the democratic wishes of its people or our own often asserted desire for social reform. This is why it will breed a whole new generation of revolutionaries in the hemisphere, driving the youth to despair of peaceful change and contempt for the Alliance for Progress. This is how we create what we fear.

Chapter Three:

Fifth Columnists

Fifth columnist is a recently coined term. It' dates only from the Spanish Civil War of 1936–1939 when the rebel General Francisco Franco announced an offensive to capture the capital of Madrid. Four columns would advance on Madrid, he said, and when the proper moment arrived a fifth column would rise within the city itself. Thus, *fifth columnist* came to mean *the enemy at home* and historians have employed the term in reference to similar movements elsewhere.

The idea of the fifth column is also a modern phenomenon. Before the French Revolutionary vision of the nation in arms caught the Western imagination, no warmaker sought or expected domestic support for his foreign adventures. Wars were the business of rulers and professional armies, not peoples. Governments did not derive their powers from the people and were relatively uninterested in the people's opinion of the government's actions. In democratic countries, however, popular support of wars is a necessity. As a result, democracies in war exert a compelling pressure on their citizens for patriotic consensus. Americans have been particularly sensitive to real or imagined domestic enemies.

There is thus a serious problem involved in using the term *fifth columnist* in connection with American history. Political abuse of the word in the interest of wartime patriotism has rendered precise definition all but impossible. As far as enthusiastic supporters of American wars are concerned, those who oppose the wars, whatever their reasons, aid the enemy through their lack of patriotism and are therefore no better than traitors. The northerner who hesitated to rally to the Union standard during the Civil War ran the risk of being branded a *copperhead,* or pro-southerner. Pro-war politicians during World War I referred to members of the anti-war IWW as "Imperial Wilhelm's Warriors" and many Americans believed that the Kaiser paid the union to sabotage the American war effort. If this notion was ludicrous, other patriotic excesses during the First World War were shameful: patriots harassed Americans with German names simply because of their ancestors' national origin. In the Cold War the practice of dubbing any critic of American bellicosity as a "communist" was and is widespread. Even pacifists who categorically reject the use of violence have been accused of being foreign agents.

Even outside this realm of hysteria it is difficult to devise any workable definition of *fifth columnist* because American pro-enemy sentiment has been strongest in the nation's two great domestic conflicts, the Revolution and the Civil War. John Adams estimated that fully one-third of the inhabitants of the thirteen colonies supported the British cause during the Revolution. To whom were they traitors? They were merely standing for values thought praiseworthy until 1776. During the secession crisis of 1861, in the border states of Kentucky and Virginia, the Confederate and Union armies successfully recruited men in the same small towns. Brothers occasionally enlisted in opposing armies. Which ones were the traitors? There were many Confederate sympathizers in Indiana, Ohio, and Illinois. Many citizens of Tennessee, Texas, and even Alabama actively took up arms on behalf of the Union. Union General George H. Thomas, the "Rock of Chickamauga," was from Confederate Virginia. Was he a traitor to the Confederacy?

The victorious Union tacitly concluded after the war that it was inexpedient to apply the concept of treason to the defeated South and tried neither rebel nor northern copperhead for the crime. Few American governments since have been so circumspect although, ironically, fifth columnists have never since been nearly so significant as the copperheads.

The Revolutionary Period

While John Adams' estimate of the number of Loyalist colonists was probably too high, a large proportion of the population did indeed support the British cause. The Loyalists were drawn chiefly but not entirely from the upper and middle classes. In the Carolinas, for example, frontiersmen traditionally hostile to the aristocrats of the tidewater (who joined the revolt as a rule) fought on behalf of the British. Governor Dunmore of Virginia organized a large Loyalist force under his command early in the war, including some slaves who were offered freedom if they deserted their patiot masters and enlisted with the Governor. Other important colonists like Massachusetts Governor Thomas Hutchinson remained loyal to Great Britain as did Benjamin Franklin's son. And the cities of New York and Philadelphia, under British control through much of the war, had large populations which were none too happy to see the departure of the "hated redcoats."

In fact, a great many Americans left with the British troops. About 100,000 colonials, a considerable number in a population of 2.5 million, fled their homes for Canada or England after the rebel victory. Most of the new states disenfranchised Loyalists, barred them from the professions and public office, or expropriated their property. It is impossible to determine exactly the value of the confiscated property, but the British government later compensated Loyalists in the amount of over £3 million sterling, a huge sum.

Fifth columnists of sorts sat in high places during the war scares of the 1790's. Edmund Randolph (1753–1813)—the son of a Loyalist—was accused while serving as Secretary of State of accepting money from the French for the purpose of embroiling the United States in a war with Great Britain. While Randolph was apparently innocent of blatant corruption in the matter, there is no doubt that he voiced the French viewpoint in President Washington's cabinet. Alexander Hamilton (1755–1804), Secretary of the Treasury under Washington, may have been guilty of similar collusion with the British.

No Americans seem to have looked fondly on the interests of the Barbary Pirates against whom an expedition was launched in 1801. The nearest thing to a fifth column during the Jeffersonian era was the outer fringe of the movement which opposed the War of 1812. While most of the New Englanders who resented that war were interested not in England's but in New England's interests, some did consider the possibility of *rapprochement* with the mother country.

The Civil War

Active pro-enemy movements emerged again clearly only with the Civil War. The draft riots in New York City were motivated in part by sympathy for the southern cause in the sense that the rioters supported the Confederate position on slavery. But the copperheads of the Midwest provide a more articulate example.

A great deal of historical debate has centered on the nature of the copperhead movement. One argument runs that they were frank pro-southerners who looked for at least a peace on Confederate terms and who would not have been chagrined by a Confederate victory. Another viewpoint argues that the copperheads were primarily concerned with domestic economic and political issues and that their southern sympathies were only apparent. At any rate, they provided a troublesome anti-war opposition to the Union government, especially in the southern sections of Ohio, Indiana, and Illinois, areas which had been settled largely by southerners. These regions frequently elected public officials who spoke stridently against the Union's prosecution of the war; the most famous of them was Clement L. Vallandigham (1820–1871) of Ohio. Sentenced to prison for speaking in favor of the Confederate cause, Vallandigham's sentence was commuted to banishment behind the Confederate lines. He stayed only briefly in the South, moving instead to Canada. From exile he was nominated by the Democratic Party for governor of Ohio and, despite his absence, barely lost the election.

Copperhead sentiment was more slight farther north, but even Wisconsin, called "the Massachusetts of the West" for its devotion to Union principles, produced Marcus "Brick" Pomeroy, the editor of the *La Crosse Democrat* who inveighed against the Union's war. Along with other copperheads Pomeroy took the position that while the South's secession was a grave error, the section had been forced to its desperate measure by northern provocations. After the Union adopted the abolition of slavery as a war aim, Pomeroy stated that the Confederacy was entirely "in the right." In far-off California several small pro-Confederate communities "seceded" from the Union and there was talk of forming an independent Pacific Coast republic.

Pro-Unionists in the South were rarely so vocal as Pomeroy and Vallandigham but there was, in fact, a great deal of opposition to secession and sympathy for the Union in the Confederacy. Anti-Confederate groups were especially powerful in eastern Tennessee, western North Carolina and Virginia, and northern Alabama and Mississippi. These areas were dominated by small, non–slaveholding farmers who could see no reason to defend their political masters, the planters. The western counties of Virginia seceded to organize the loyal state of West Virginia. Union armies did not have to conquer eastern Tennessee. The troops were greeted as liberators by the citizenry, a fifth column such as Generalissimo Franco never found in Madrid. The political hero of eastern Tennessee was Andrew Johnson who refused to secede with his state in 1861 and remained in the Union government. Northern Alabama and Mississippi were similar regions. According to a local legend, one county "seceded" from Mississippi to form the "Republic of Jones."

These hilly lands were not only settled by non-slaveholding farmers, they were isolated and fast, difficult places in which to establish political control if the population was hostile. The hills also served as a refuge for deserters from the Confederate Army who sometimes organized into little bands which harassed Confederate troops and foraged the countryside. While the proportion of deserters from the Union Army was as high as in the South, the problem never assumed the proportions of a major nuisance in the less rugged terrain of the Union. There were no such bandit bands to divert the attention of the regular army behind the Union's lines.

But the Confederacy's most damaging fifth column was the black population of the section. The slave insurrection which some northerners hoped for never materialized. Most slaves worked loyally on their plantations as long as the war was remote. But when Union troops reached the neighborhood, slaves fled to the Union lines in great numbers and many of the men enlisted readily in the Army.

The World Wars

Many Americans who had emigrated from the German and Austro-Hungarian Empires were decidedly not cordial to their adopted land's war against their mother countries in 1917. But, perhaps because of an awareness of the patriotic hysteria loose in the land, these groups kept silent during World War I and took no fifth-columnist action. It is one of the peculiarities of the war that, although there was great popular fear of subversion and sabotage, the actual amount of pro-enemy activity was insignificant.

Pro-fascist sentiment was common in the United States during the months before the nation entered World War II. Several Italian-American organizations admired the Italian dictator, Benito Mussolini, and took pride in Italy's apparent military power. A more sinister phenomenon was the admiration of Adolf Hitler which flourished among some German-Americans and many non-Germans as well. The German-American Bund, centered chiefly in New York City, aped Hitler's paramilitary elite corps with jackboots, jodphurs, and bully tactics; William Dudley Pelley of North Carolina molded an organization of Silver Shirts to propagate Nazi views. The popular radio voice, Father Charles Coughlin, turned increasingly from economic discussions to the Nazi brand of anti-Semitism during the late thirties and early forties.

Whatever the nature of these activities before the United States joined the European war, they were inconsequential during the conflict. Organizations like the Bund and the Silver Shirts were quickly dismantled after the declaration of war and, if they functioned underground, were more ridiculous than dangerous. Pro-Nazi publications shut down their presses or reversed their lines and Father Coughlin's ecclesiastical superior ordered him off the airways within a few months. Moreover, the federal government gave overt American Nazis scant opportunity to practice any fifth-columnist activities. In a series of trials that provided no better examples of legal due process than the World War I prosecutions of Wobblies had done, the government focussed the nation's attention on alleged pro-Germans.

The worst-treated "fifth columnists" of the period were not fifth columnists at all. These were the tens of thousands of Japanese-Americans, or Nisei, primarily on the West Coast, who were herded into concentration camps shortly after the attack on Pearl Harbor and stripped of their property and legal rights on the sole basis that they were of Japanese descent. This was one of the shabbiest chapters in the history of American racism and civil liberties. Even the harassments of German-Americans during World War I were private affairs from which the government was officially disassociated. But this was the government itself taking the initiative. Many of the abused Nisei were descended from several generations of American citizens and subsequent investigation, after the harm had been done, proved there was no danger whatsoever of fifth-columnist activities among Japanese-Americans.

There has been no repetition of the affair, perhaps because America's involvement in the Cold War has been, until recently, a popular foreign policy. Some social critics of the fifties, however, pointed out that the government quietly keeps some of the old concentration camps in a state of readiness. With the growth of a domestic left wing which frankly supports social revolutions abroad which the government is engaged in fighting, the camps may be used again.

Loyalists in the Revolution*

Leonard W. Labaree

In this short excerpt from *Conservatism in Early American History,* a famous historian of colonial America, Leonard Woods Labaree, discusses the economic sources of Loyalism during the American Revolution. It is important to realize, however, that Labaree did not regard Loyalism as a purely economic phenomenon. He also analyzed in depth the psychological and religious sources of the movement.

The Revolution was in part a civil conflict between fellow Americans who disagreed on the solution of their current problems. There were those who were willing from the start to use extreme measures to resist the decisions of the home [English] government. There were those who objected to the policies of the ministry but counseled moderation and were drawn in to support the radicals only when the course of events seemed to leave them no other choice. There were still others—and these constituted a very large part of the total population—who wanted to take no part in the controversy, one way or the other, and hoped only to be left alone to pursue their own lives in peace and quiet. And lastly there was a substantial minority who in the end took sides with the British against their fellow colonials. These last were, in general, the men of conservative temperament in whom we are chiefly interested here.

Colonial conservatives might—as most of them actually did—believe that Britain was pursuing a mistaken policy in beginning to tax the colonies by act of Parliament. Here was an innovation, on principle quite as distressing to a colonial conservative as to a radical. But when the reaction to the parliamentary and ministerial measures went beyond the stage of respectful protest and led to civil disobedience and violence, some of the colonials drew back. When civil disobedience was followed by armed resistance, and then by a declaration of independence, and these were accompanied by an internal revolution in the institutions of colonial society itself, many Americans found themselves supporting the mother country. Not only was Britain the rightful claimant to their allegiance, but she was the only agency that could be relied on to restore society to its proper foundations. Therefore, they sided with Great Britain. By contemporary Americans such men were bitterly called *Tories;* by their proud descendants in Canada

---

* From Leonard W. Labaree, *Conservatism in American History* (New York: New York University Press, 1948). Used by permission.

and elsewhere and by a more understanding generation of Americans today they are more often referred to as *Loyalists*.

. . . .

In many cases, it is clear, men sided with the British government because it seemed to their personal advantage to do so. Such motives were especially obvious among members of the ruling class and particularly among royal or proprietary office-holders. These men had a vested interest, partly economic and partly social and psychological, in the maintenance of political leadership and in the prestige as well as the material rewards that went with public office. In large measure (although with many individual exceptions) direction and control of the revolutionary movement, which was originally in the hands of the accustomed political spokesmen, tended to pass in the course of time to men of little or no previous distinction or political importance. Their assumption of leadership, as well as the tactics they employed, alienated many a colonial notable who was not accustomed to seeing political power exercised by members of what he called the "mob." In this connection I have tried as one test case to discover just what proportion of the members of the royal and proprietary councils at the outbreak of the war ought to be classed as Loyalists, either moderate or extreme. There did not prove to be enough accurate information to permit an exact statistical statement, but it would appear from the available evidence that from one-half to two-thirds of the councilors either openly espoused the British cause or were placed on parole by the Whigs as disaffected persons.

A large proportion of the administrative officers took the British side. Their action is easily understandable. Many were British-born and lived in America only because their jobs were here. Practically all stood to lose their salaries if the colonies became independent. Williams Eddis, royal surveyor of the customs and proprietary commissioner of the loan office in Maryland, expressed well the attitude of his fellow officeholders when he wrote soon after the Declaration of Independence:

> I wish well to America—it is my duty—my inclination so to do—but I cannot—I will not—consent to act in direct opposition to my oath of allegiance and my deliberate opinion. Rather than submit to a conduct so base, so inconsistent with my principles, I will give up all—embrace ruin!—and trust to the protecting care of Providence for the future disposition of me and mine.[1]

---

[1] William Eddis, *Letters from America, Historical and Descriptive: Comprising Occurrences from 1769, to 1777, Inclusive* (London: 1792), p. 217.

Self-interest also played a part in determining the attitude of many of the great landowners and merchants. They were the leading men of property in the colonies with the most to lose from an upheaval in the orderly processes of society as it was constituted. These were the classes of men who, over the years, had tended to show the most consistent conservatism on other issues that challenged their economic or political leadership. It is not surprising, therefore, that from these groups there should emerge a large proportion of men who resisted the changes in society and the attack upon their control which the revolutionary movement threatened to produce.

Among such men, the position and attitude of the colonial merchants has received much scholarly attention.[2] In the early stages of the dispute with Britain many of these men were active leaders in the opposition to the mother country. It was the merchants themselves who brought about the first non-importation agreements. Several of them, later distinguished as Loyalists, were elected to the Stamp Act Congress [1775]. It took time for these men to see that they had started something they could not stop and finally could not even control. At first they apparently did not object greatly to the somewhat boisterous popular demonstrations against British acts. As Carl Becker has effectively put it,

> a little rioting was well enough, so long as it was directed to the one end of bringing the English government to terms. But when the destruction of property began to be relished for its own sake by those who had no property and the cry of liberty came loudest from those who were without political privilege, it was time to call a halt. These men might not cease their shouting when purely British restrictions were removed.[3]

Many a man who joined heartily in the first steps of organized protest came to regret his acts. Many an essentially conservative colonial discovered to his dismay that he had unwittingly cast himself in the role of Pandora.

Some merchants were more cautious from the start. John Watts, a leading businessman of New York, for example, objected to the

---

[2] The outstanding work is, of course, Arthur M. Schlesinger's *The Colonial Merchants and the American Revolution* (New York: Columbia University Press, 1918). Also important are Charles M. Andrews, "The Boston Merchants and the Non-Importation Movement," *Publications* of the Colonial Society of Massachusetts, XIX (Boston: 1918), 159–259; and Virginia D. Harrington, *The New York Merchant on the Eve of the Revolution* (New York: Columbia University Press, 1935).

[3] Carl L. Becker, *The History of Political Parties in the Province of New York, 1760–1776* (Madison: University of Wisconsin Press, 1909), p. 31.

Stamp Act but wrote a friend in November 1765 that he believed no prudent man should meddle with the question of parliamentary taxation except among friends as a mere matter of speculation. "The less is said on the subject," he added, "the better on this side; 'tis too delicate if not presumptuous."[4] There were others who felt as Watts did and later could pride themselves on their consistent behavior. Whether a merchant was an active instigator of non-importation agreements or one who refused to take any steps in the face of injurious British legislation, he was likely before long to feel that the chief threat to his prosperity and to the principle of property rights came not from the British Parliament but from the colonial radicals. With the exception of those merchants who engaged largely in smuggling, their class depended for their business chiefly on the orderly conduct of overseas trade. Economic boycott was an effective but a highly expensive weapon; experience with it led many merchants to regret their public-spirited adherence to the non-importation agreements.

What in many cases was quite as important as the immediate financial loss which the merchants suffered in the dispute was the changed attitude of the lower classes. In this matter the other men of property, especially the landed gentry in the North, joined the merchants. The *vulgar* had found a new sport, the destruction of property. A man like John Watts might deplore the burning of Lieutenant Governor Colden's coach by the Stamp Act rioters, but he would not be too upset about it, for he detested Colden personally. But when, nearly five years later, a midnight mob seized and burned some goods which the New York merchants' Committee of Inspection had sequestered for violation of the non-importation agreement, such merchants as Isaac Low, head of the committee, were outraged. He and his fellow committeemen denounced the act as "a high insult" to themselves and the city and branded the perpetrators as "lawless ruffians."[5] And when in 1773 the "Indians" of Boston dumped £15,000 worth of tea into the harbor, and the next year citizens of Maryland publicly burned the tea ship *Peggy Stewart*, owned by Annapolis merchants, it became perfectly clear to men of wealth and standing that the sacred right of property was under attack. Men of this class came to believe that it had been a mistake to sanction agitation against authority in the first place. Now authority had to be supported if their own property

---

[4] Dorothy C. Barck (ed.), *Letter Book of John Watts, Merchant and Councillor of New York, January 1, 1762–December 22, 1765* (Collections of the New York Historical Society; New York: 1928).

[5] Schlesinger, *Colonial Merchants and the American Revolution*, p. 190.

were to be safeguarded. In such terms many men began to see the issues of the times and, accordingly, chose to uphold the Crown in their own self-interest.

The Proclamation of Emancipation (1863)

Samuel Medary

The Crisis was a newspaper published in Columbus, Ohio by Samuel Medary for the specific purpose of publicizing Medary's copperhead views on the sectional crisis. This editorial from *The Crisis* for January 7, 1863 is a good example of the effect of the Emancipation Proclamation on the copperheads. With the abolition of slavery clearly a war aim, anti-Negro sentiment in the North was galvanized into a significant movement. The first half of 1863, between the Proclamation and the Confederate defeats at Gettysburg and Vicksburg, found this fifth-columnist movement at its peak.

This Proclamation, under pretense of setting free four millions of Negroes, strikes at the independence of every state in the Union.

It creates a dictatorship at Washington, and subjects persons and property to the will and whims of one man, irrespective of constitutional laws. It overrides juries and all legislative authority.

It changes the rights of property, and subjects all contracts, deeds or record, mode and compensation of labor to the arbitrary will of bayonets and military rule.

It changes the whole relationship of the states with each other, and of the general government of the states.

It revolutionizes at one dash of the pen our form of government, and transfers the white race from freedom to absolute despotism.

It palliates and justifies secessionism, and places us of the North in the wrong, by raising the issue of revolution against usurpation and a central despotism.

It converts the war into one to destroy, instead of to save the Union, and is thus a foul wrong to every soldier in the Army who seized his musket under patriotic impulses.

It stamps the government and the war orators with the open lie, who raised armies under false pretenses and with lies in their mouths.

It is as impudent and insulting to God as to man, for it declares those equal whom God created unequal.

It not only assumes to rule man, but to correct the "errors" of the Almighty.

It changes the whole status of the white and the black races, and commands the white soldier to be a slave in arms to the Negro.

It subjects the command and action of the army to the will and demand of the Negro, and it must be obeyed.

It is a proclamation bidding for insurrection and servile war by the blacks, and the extermination of the white race—even of the women and children—and hence is a disgrace to civilization for which we must all bear more or less of the stigma.

It leaves the North with no hope of any possible reconciliation with the South ever again, unless they at once, and in tones of indignant thunder, from every press and every rostrum, denounce in the most emphatic manner their abhorrence of the guilty act, and wash their skirts clean of every stain of its contamination.

It joins issue in a political, moral, religious sense with every Union-loving man of the North; and the gauntlet being thus cast at our feet, we are less worthy of freedom than the Negro, whom this Proclamation pretends to benefit, if we do not take it up without stint of words or suppression of indignant feeling.

Confederate Lovers of the Union (1866)

Henry Stuart Foote

Henry Stuart Foote served through most of the Civil War in the Confederate Congress where he was President Jefferson Davis' chief critic. Called the "Vallandigham of the Confederacy," he fled into the Union lines in 1865. The next year he published a book called *The War of the Rebellion; or Scylla and Charbydis . . . The Causes and Consequences of the Late Civil War.** In this chapter he expresses the views of the southern loyalists on the Confederate handling of the secession crisis. It is a bitter attack.

. . . Mr. Davis and his official associates had no correct conception of the true character and dimensions of the war into which they had so hastily plunged, as was afterward frankly confessed in many a lugubrious harangue, and in more than one solemn official document.

* (New York: Harper & Brothers, 1866).

They did not believe at first that the conflict would endure for a twelve-month, and were even weak enough to calculate most confidently upon strong *northern aid,* which it is now well known there never was the least probability of their receiving; albeit ex-President Pierce and several others, whose letters to Mr. Davis have recently seen the light, had plied this confiding personage with secret promises of support, upon which he built in part his hopes of one day wielding an imperial sceptre. As to the interposition of *foreign* powers in behalf of the now warring states of the South, though many deceitful assurances were received from abroad at different periods of the contest, no man of sound intellect anywhere now supposes that either the French or English government ever seriously thought of embroiling itself in a transatlantic feud, the formal enlistment in which would, in all probability, bring upon itself swift and assured destruction. Mr. Davis evidently thought far otherwise when he said at Jackson, Mississippi, just before leaving his own home for the city of Montgomery, "England would not allow our great staple to be damned up within our present limits; the starving thousands in their midst would not allow it. We have nothing to apprehend from blockade. But, if they attempt invasion by land, we must take the war *out of our territory.* If war must come, it must be upon northern, and not upon southern soil." Continuing to talk in this menacing strain along the road to Montgomery, when he reached Stevenson, an important railroad point, he said:

> Your border states will gladly come into the southern Confederacy within sixty days, as *we will be their only* friends. England will recognize us, and a glorious future is before us. The grass will grow in the northern cities, where the pavements have been worn off by the tread of commerce. We will carry war where it is easy to advance—where food for the *sword* and *torch* await our armies in the densely-populated cities; and though they (the enemy) may come and spoil our crops, we can raise them as before, while they can not rear the cities which took years of industry and millions of money to build.

It was evidently, in part, under the inspiration of such speeches as these from his executive chief, that the war secretary, Mr. Walker, on the night after the storming of Fort Sumter, announced that "the Confederate flag would soon be seen flying from the top of the Capitol in Washington."

.   .   .   .

It must ever appear to men at all given to philosophic meditation upon the concerns of government, and who have made themselves in the least degree familiar with great historic examples, exceedingly surprising that the secession leaders at this perilous crisis (all of whom professed a profound regard alike for the corporate rights of the states as for general popular freedom) should have failed to discover the extreme dangers to both of these which a continued state of war must engender. All professed writers on government, from Aristotle down to Calhoun, have pointed out these dangers, and some of them have expatiated with great force upon the inevitable tendency of belligerent measures to *centralize* all civil power in a single hand. They have taught us that if the state of war be continued too long, nothing but the greatest circumspection on the part of those interested in preserving freedom can prevent the building up of an irresponsible despotism. And this tendency to *centralization* has, confessedly, always been more observable in such wars as are waged by one portion of the citizens of a free country against citizens of kindred blood, of the same country and lineage, upon the natal soil common to them both. It would be easy to specify the efficient causes of this, and quite as easy to illustrate and support the stated proposition by numerous instances in point. It is Mr. Webster, I think, who, in some one of his majestic orations, likens the action of the governmental machine in times of civil commotion to the chariot wheels of antiquity, which are described as taking fire from the celerity of their own motion. Two such machines, in close proximity, igniting from the same cause, must each serve, by a natural reciprocation of power, to increase the general combustion. It would have been scarcely possible to preserve a well balanced federative system either in the North or in the South while such a war as that from which we have just so happily escaped was in fierce and ever-varying progress. Had peaceful secession even turned out to be a practicable experiment, the danger of constantly recurring border wars would have demanded the location of considerable bodies of defensive soldiery along the line of territorial separation on the one side and on the other of that line, in order to guard against hostile incursions, ever possible to occur. These military bands would have soon grown into standing armies of great and constantly accumulating strength, until each of them would, as so often has been the case heretofore, have given to the country which should have thus fallen under its control an imperial master, or would, at least, have decreed the establishment of a government far stronger in its frame than that of the republican form has ever been heretofore adjudged to be. But a separation effected by the sword must have been fraught with yet greater peril. A long and arduous struggle between two segments of the same republic, marked by the copious shedding of the blood of valued citizens on either side, would necessarily have engendered rancors exceedingly difficult to be allayed, even after hostilities should have ceased to be prosecuted. These rancors, during the season of hostilities, would have been constantly multiplying and increasing in intensity. The ordinary expedients of war would have become, in the estimation of the parties struggling for superiority, far too gentle and ineffective for the fierce and hellish purposes of a wrathful and all-desolating vengeance. The infernal furies themselves would be called in by mutual and trumpet-toned entreaties, to swell the thrice tragic scene of general social ruin. *Sicilian Vespers*, or *Feasts of St. Bartholomew*,* would have ceased to awaken their accustomed horror when confronting such scenes as those to which our own loved country was, only a month or two since, in danger of falling a prey. A state of things so appalling as that described would, of necessity, have demanded that large and latitudinous powers should be vested in the executive department of the government, wheresoever situated, in order to regulate and hold in some little restraint, if possible, all those potent elements of mischief. In order to prevent universal anarchy, universal butchery, and wide-sweeping crimes of every sort, the organization of a despotism would have become a fatal necessity. Such vast powers, once trusted in the hands of any man less virtuous than Washington himself, it would be absurd to expect would be *voluntarily* surrendered, and to tear them from so potential a depository by *force* might perchance be found impossible.

The War Hypnosis (1940)

William Dudley Pelley, the head of a Nazi organization called the Silver Shirts, published from Asheville, North Carolina during the late thirties and early forties a magazine entitled the *Weekly Liberation*. The magazine was described on its masthead as "A Journal of unorthodox comment on world affairs ... espousing a more equitable economy for the United States at home

---

* Sicilian Vespers is the name of a bloody uprising that occurred in 1282, during which Sicilian rebels slaughtered their erstwhile French overlords. The Massacre (or Feast) of St. Bartholomew involved the death of some 50,000 French Protestants (Huguenots) at the hands of the Catholic nobility in 1572.

and a non-meddlesome sovereignty abroad, both contained in the Newer Statesmanship of each country's working out the destiny which Divine Providence has allotted it by fiat of wholesome racial performance." This distilled in practice to unstinting admiration of Adolf Hitler (who was described playfully as "efficient Adolf"), Anglophobia, and anti-Semitism. This article, from the *Weekly Liberation* for July 7, 1940, was typical of the magazine's viewpoint. The original title was "Behind the Hypnosis."

It seems to be given only to a few thousand people, scattered across the United States, to know accurately what the real state of affairs is in Europe. The millions of Americans are tragically unaware that almost all dispatches coming from overseas and published by the great press associations are either British-manufactured or British-censored, otherwise they are quietly doctored or lost along the cable route. Germany cracks this censorship to a degree by using the radio to "tell the world" what is happening with the Axis partners. If the American people only knew the *true* story of European and English conditions, it is improbable that they would for a moment espouse billions squandered in their assumed defense.

To read the reports out of London, one would imagine that the war was going excellently with England and that thrashing Germany is but a matter of time. But actually the war is costing Great Britain $38 million per day, figured in American dollars, in addition to a financially stricken condition almost as bad as the United States' under Roosevelt. Sir Kingsley Wood, chancellor of the exchequer, told the Commons this week that he wanted a vote of credit of $4 billion more— the sum again figured in American dollars—and that additional taxes must be raised on top of already high levies that have brought the cost of English living something like 60 per cent over what it was last summer before the war broke out. Of the $38 million a day that Britain is spending to keep up the Churchill murderbust, 26 million is going to direct support of the army, navy, and air force. This money is being provided by bonds on the kosher interest system, whereas Germany owes herself nothing. Yet the propagandists have the gall to assure all and sundry that the Nazis are due to bust first. One wonders how.

Another favorite ruse to bolster up the world's courage till America can be drawn in to serve English purposes, is announcement of the "terrible" conditions prevailing in those countries conquered by the sundry blitzkriegs. So atrocious is the mass hypnosis outside of Europe that the slightest attempt to report the truth is frenziedly blasted as German propaganda. Journalists court extinction as fifth columnists for daring it. The other day newspapermen from neutral countries were invited over into Slovakia to poke, pry, and observe for themselves just how terrible conditions were, under the Nazi protectorate. They could send out anything they pleased—provided England would let it be cabled overseas. Later, the Germans gave a reception to the scribblers at which the Dutch journalist, Leo von Heinigen, correspondent of one of the "conquered" countries, publicly admitted that Slovakia appeared to be more free now than it ever had been under Jewish rule as a stooge of France. "We are convinced that the Slovakian people can develop their own state politically, industrially and culturally as they wish," was the substance of his confession. But did you see anything about it in your American newspapers? Whether one likes Hitler or does not like Hitler, what has any of it to do with facts about true European conditions being allowed to reach Americans? Some day Americans are going to find the truth out anyhow. The neutral newsmen could find nothing wrong with new conditions in Slovakia, so the fact wasn't news.

The disgust of the really neutral American prompts a paraphrase of the anecdote—

"I've got a perfect news story!" exclaimed an excited newspaperman.

"A man bit a dog!" guessed his friend.

"Naw, a bull threw Winston Churchill."

Chapter Four:

The Vietnam War

The Background of the War

Like the war itself, the American people's awareness of their nation's involvement in the affairs of Vietnam developed slowly, in individually imperceptible steps. That involvement actually began in 1945 when the United States concurred in the restoration of French rule in Indochina following the defeat of Japanese hegemony there. The Vietnamese have a national history older than any European people but the country had been a French colony since the mid–nineteenth century. France surrendered the colony to Japan without a battle in 1940 and French forces actually assisted in the Japanese administration of the colony. But throughout the Second World War Vietnamese nationalists under the leadership of Ho Chi Minh harassed the Japanese and, by 1945, were the only force in the country which could claim both the loyalty of the inhabitants and a record clean of collaboration with the Japanese.

During the war, Ho Chi Minh secured Allied promises of autonomy for Vietnam after the fighting. But, as the outlines of the Cold War took shape in 1945 and 1946, the United States agreed with Britain and France to the recolonization of the region. The Western nations were hypersensitive to Communist expansion in the postwar years and Ho Chi Minh was a Communist. He had been one of the founders of the French Communist Party in 1920 and never severed his ties with the movement.

With French power reestablished behind the puppet emperor Bao Dai, Ho Chi Minh regrouped his guerrillas into an anti-French movement, the Vietminh. French forces held the major and minor cities of the country but much of the countryside was loyal to the Vietminh. The guerrillas steadily chipped away at French power until, in 1953, the French resolved to join conclusive battle with the rebels by arming an "impregnable" fortress in the heart of hostile territory, at Dien Bien Phu. Vietnamese forces under General Giap attacked the fort and, after a siege which lasted the better part of a year, stunned the world by capturing the huge garrison. The United States had aided the French with money and material, but Dien Bien Phu was still a French ignominy.

The United States intervened directly only after the Geneva Conference of 1954 which ostensibly settled the question of Vietnam's future. For the purposes of expediting French withdrawal, the country was divided into two zones of occupation. The Vietminh would occupy the northern half of the country, the French the southern half. Vietnam would be reunified after general elections to be held no later than 1956. While the United States did not sign the Geneva Accords, American Secretary of State John Foster Dulles announced that his country would honor them.

The elections of 1956 were never held. The French hurriedly withdrew before the terminal date and left the southern half of the country to the government of Ngo Dinh Diem. Diem was not, like Bao Dai, a collaborator of the French. He had opposed French rule and spent the final years of the colonial regime in exile. But this in itself was not enough to recommend Diem to the Vietnamese. He was a member of the Mandarin class and partial to the interests of Vietnam's reactionary landlords, a hated class of men. Diem was also a Roman Catholic in a country where Catholics were the traditional favorites of the French while the overwhelming majority of the population was Buddhist. Finally, Diem was a petty autocrat who employed terror in parts of the country to aid landlords in collecting rents, sometimes in areas where the peasants had long since redistributed the land.

It was with the coming of Diem that the United States was fatefully involved in Vietnam. Diem had spent part of his exile in America and owed his establishment in Saigon to American influence. The United States dispatched soldiers to Vietnam as advisors to Diem's army and flooded his treasury with financial aid. Thus, whether or not the American government was directly responsible for Diem's refusal to hold elections in 1956, the United States was inevitably drawn into the consequences of that act. American military advisors became combat soldiers when, within two years, South Vietnamese peasants initiated guerrilla warfare against Diem's government.

The National Liberation Front (the military arm of which has been dubbed the *Vietcong*) was organized in 1960 and claimed to be the sole legitimate government of the southern half of the country. The Front included representatives of most of the country's religious and economic groups although it was dominated by Communists, a fact Diem used to good advantage when describing his war. The NLF was more than a worthy adversary to Diem, actually governing much of the country. It was popular with the peasantry while Diem's corrupt troops were disliked, and its men were easily the better soldiers. The NLF captured great quantities of American arms from the South Vietnamese army and, indeed, many individual guerrillas were American-trained: the South

Vietnamese desertion rate was phenomenal and, while many deserters simply went home, many others joined the Vietcong.

Diem's control of the country was already shaky by 1960 and, despite an increase in American assistance under President John F. Kennedy, toppled in 1963 when a junta of generals assassinated Diem and his retainers. The key year of the American intervention was 1963. With Diem's removal, the South Vietnamese government was very weak and would probably have fallen easily to the NLF had not the United States been present. A succession of mediocre leaders seized the government, each soon displaced by a new aspirant. Only with the ascendancy in 1965 of a former pilot for the French air force, Nguyen Cao Ky, did this comic phase draw to a close. In the meantime, the NLF had established its control over most of rural South Vietnam.

Nineteen sixty-three was also the year of President Kennedy's assassination. While Kennedy was responsible for the massive American presence in Vietnam, his successor, Lyndon B. Johnson, altered its nature. Kennedy and his advisors banked on the premise that the Saigon government could win the loyalty of the South Vietnamese people. Under Johnson, however, with the political war in a shambles, the United States came to rely more completely on military power. The war was soon almost entirely an American affair. United States troops fought the guerrillas while South Vietnamese troops assumed duties behind the lines. President Johnson also emphasized as never before the position that the war was not a civil war but a war of invasion by North Vietnamese. He ordered an air war against the North in order to halt the "infiltration." Ironically, where there had been little North Vietnamese intervention to that point, regulars from the North soon poured across the border in the thousands.

The piecemeal increase of America's involvement in Vietnam introduced a new term to military nomenclature: *escalation*. The American effort (and the NLF–North Vietnamese responses) increased in seemingly insignificant steps—*escalated*. The manpower commitment crept quietly from a few dozen men to a few hundred to a few thousand to ten thousand to a half million. The activities of American personnel escalated too: they were first merely advisors, then defenders of American bases, then combat soldiers; next there were retaliatory bombing raids against the North, and then there was saturation-bombing of North and South Vietnam which exceeded the total of American bombing during World War II. Each step was accompanied by assurances that it was all that was needed to win the war. Americans discovered only belatedly that they were involved in a major military venture. Critics of the war wondered whether the escalation was a symptom of governmental stupidity or a calaculated campaign to ease Americans painlessly into a full scale war against communism.

The Growth of a Peace Movement

The movement in opposition to the war also escalated. A few voices during the 1950's warned that the United States was involved in a potentially dangerous situation. With President Kennedy's first massive intervention, isolated groups of college-student radicals began to question the American policy and to attack specific government allegations about the nature of the war. The early movement was a lark. The much-praised Diem government was so patently corrupt that it seemed to the protesters but a matter of months before a popular outcry forced American withdrawal. American support of the *opera-bouffe* governments which followed Diem seemed more ludicrous than sinister. Protesters laughed more than they worried.

The early anti-war movement was a collegiate movement and characteristically chose as its medium the *teach-in*. Teach-ins were meetings of students, professors, and interested individuals, half lecture and seminar, half political rally. The meetings studied Vietnamese history and debated American policy. The rationale of the movement was education: if the fallacy of the government's line could be demonstrated, protesters believed, the government would be forced to reverse its stand. Teach-ins varied in size from meetings of a few dozen people at small colleges to gatherings of thousands at large universities.

By 1964, within a year after the fall of Diem, the teach-in approach quietly died. It had created the best-informed mass movement in American history but Washington proved uninterested in the movement's findings. Nor did the majority of Americans notice the critiques and alternatives offered by the movement. And Vietnamese events in the wake of Diem's fall, conclusive proof of their argument so far as the protesters were concerned, were all but ignored in the larger society.

The anti-war movement escalated to demonstrations. If dialogue did not move Washington, protesters reasoned, political pressure might. The size of the movement had been augmented by the interest of churchmen and civil rights activists, liberals disenchanted by deviations from Kennedy's policy, many middle-class people never before politically active, and militant Negro groups, especially Black Power advocates. The movement was still strongest in the colleges and universities but no longer restricted to them.

Demonstrations ranged from handfuls of Women's Strike for Peace activists standing vigil on the streets of small towns and hundreds of students at campus rallies to marches by hundreds of thousands in the San Francisco Bay area, New York City, and Washington in 1965 and 1966. As the teach-ins educated the movement, the demonstrations swelled its numbers and infused many protesters with a willingness to act. Yet the demonstrations did not noticeably affect government policy.

The movement's greatest frustration, however, was not its inability to end the war with a picket sign. It was the fact that they felt they had destroyed the government's case and were nevertheless ignored; they had correctly predicted the course of the war yet were still shunned by the majority of the population. Many American congressmen, for example, claimed that they would never have approved the involvement in Vietnam in advance but felt obligated to make the best of the error. To the protesters this was the ultimate in political deceit. They remonstrated that they had pointed out what was going to happen in advance and continued to warn against expansions in the war which American politicians would again docilely ratify when they occurred.

Peace demonstrations escalated to resistance beginning in 1966. Individuals who had been political moderates when they first objected to the war were radicalized by the frustrations and portents of the military expansion. Absolute pacifists were the first to resist in their refusal to cooperate with the draft. The movement rallied behind such individuals as David Mitchell, who refused "to go," and soldiers who, already in the armed forces, balked at participation in the war. The government did not reveal the exact number of servicemen who quietly refused to obey orders that would ship them to Vietnam or officers who resigned over the war, although it maintained that such incidents of resistance were few. There were, however, many publicized cases to absorb the movement's attention:

—The Fort Hood Three, a trio of young soldiers who refused to embark for Vietnam; they cited as their justification the Nuremburg Trials of German war criminals, which had established the principal that individuals are morally bound to disobey a government's immoral command;

—Captain Howard Levy, a drafted army doctor who refused to give medical training to Special Forces soldiers bound for Vietnam;

—Donald Duncan, a Special Forces sergeant who left the service after ten years and denounced American actions in Vietnam;

—American prisoners freed by the NLF who endorsed the Vietnamese cause; and

—four sailors who defected first to Japan, then the Soviet Union, and then to Sweden where they were granted asylum and soon followed by dozens of others.

Flight from the U.S. to Canada or Great Britain in order to avoid the draft reached large proportions during 1965. But, to a generation of political militants, flight was unpopular. Angry opponents of the war called for mass action at home to disrupt the processes upon which the war effort depended. In late 1967 protesters attempted at Oakland, California, and New York City to shut down Selective Service induction centers by "sitting-in" at the entrances of the buildings. In less direct attacks, campus radicals harassed job interviewers from the Dow Chemical Corporation (manufacturer of napalm) and the Central Intelligence Agency (held to be the perpetrator of many American actions in Vietnam). Others pressured college administrations to cease their cooperation with the Selective Service System in classifying students for draft purposes. While Dow and the CIA were driven from many campuses and several universities severed their formal connections with Selective Service, disruption was less successful at the induction centers. Police arrested demonstrators as soon as they sealed off the buildings and, while some inductees refused to cross the briefly effective pickets, others walked over the protesters. The draft process functioned smoothly during even the largest demonstrations and over a hundred thousand protesters failed, in November, 1967, to close down the brain center of the war, the Pentagon.

The resort to resistance evidenced the movement's loss of faith in the electoral wisdom of the American public which, however passively, continued to support the war. It also illustrated the growing radicalization of the movement. Even the most conventional of protesters like Dr. Benjamin Spock (arrested in 1968 for urging draft-resistance) concluded that neither reason nor compassion would ever move the American government.

Resistance, however, also represented a measure of disintegration in the movement. The attempts to disrupt the war machinery were sometimes accompanied by violence. Most of this was initiated by police or pro-war hecklers but, for the first time, some originated with the protesters. *Agents-provocateurs* were discovered within the movement for the first time. Three activists in the Chicago movement were revealed to be agents for the Chicago police force's "intelligence squad." These were not merely spies but, as the head of the Chicago Peace Council noted, "at our meetings they invariably took the most militant positions, trying to provoke the movement from its non-violent force to the wildest kinds of ventures." Another sort of disintegration was illustrated by an incident at the Pentagon demonstration of November, 1967. A group of "hippy" devotees of a Hindu guru and an American Indian shaman attempted to levitate the building through chants and prayer bells, the guru later claiming success to the extent of a few inches. On balance, however, the surprising feature of this anti-war movement was not the erraticism of a few but the fact that, after seven years of frustration, the movement was still vital. Few American mass movements of such intensity have had such a history.

The movement was unique in the history of American anti-war groups in several other particulars—in the number of its activists, for example. While comparable numbers of Americans opposed the War of 1812, the Mexican War, and World War I, never before were hundreds of thousands willing to take to the streets so urgently. Compared to the decade that preceded it, the 1960's were years of political turmoil and the anti-war movement was at the center along with the Civil Rights protests. A majority of Americans supported the war at least through 1966. But willingness to act was on the side of the dissidents. An anti-war march in New York City early in 1967 drew 300,000 people. A retaliatory pro-war march the next week drew fewer than 25,000. In April, 1968, over 100,000 gathered in the city to protest the war while a pro-war rally the same day drew 2,000.

The movement was also distinguished by its comprehensive nature. The mass media were attracted to the colorful in their coverage of the demonstrations and their accounts led many to believe the movement was a bizarre fringe group of unkempt bohemians. In fact, the protesters were at least as heterogeneous as American society. Small town demonstrations were likely to include housewives, businessmen, doctors, dentists, ministers, and workers. Demonstrations in large cities added students, college professors, bohemians, nuns, veterans in uniform, and show-business celebrities. A number of retired generals spoke against the war as did even a handful of U.S. senators. The opponents of the War of 1812, on the contrary, were geographically centered almost entirely in New England; the opponents of the Mexican War derived from abolitionist and Free Soil movements; and the opponents of World War I were chiefly from cetain specific ethnic and politically radical groups.

Another interesting characteristic of the movement was that anti-war groups traditionally suspicious of one another cooperated remarkably closely in this cause. A conservative opponent of the war like William J. Fulbright would not, of course, collaborate with the pro-Chinese Progressive Labor Party and would not even walk in a march. But, at the movement's grassroots, anti-war groups from pacifists to liberals viewed collaboration with American Communists as far less heinous than the actions of their government and the indolence of the American people. Pacifists and political moderates saw the presence of fifth columnists in their ranks as a tactical handicap but regarded the cause of ending the war as worth the association.

The Ideology of the Opposition

The arguments against the war were as diverse as its membership. Pacifists opposed the war because they opposed all wars: war is inherently immoral; war solves nothing. Non-pacifist humanitarians objected to the intervention because, they argued, the nature of this war required American forces to be brutal beyond condonation. The United States was fighting popularly-supported guerrillas and was therefore fighting the helpless—the aged, women, and children—as well as enemy combatants. American technology meant the indiscriminate slaughter of innocents. Napalm (jellied gasoline) was dropped from the air on hapless villages from which the armed men were in fact usually absent. Hamlets were destroyed, their inhabitants removed to concentration camps and the none-too-tender mercies of the venal South Vietnamese government. The bombing of North Vietnam was often directed at schools, hospitals, and other unstrategic targets. The American destruction of Dien Bien Phu, which North Vietnam had converted into a leper colony, was pointed out as dramatic evidence of the inevitable immorality in prosecuting such a war. Any alternative, protesters argued, was preferable to the atrocities on their nation's conscience.

Other critics agreed with the government that moralism was beside the point in war. They objected to the conflict because they felt it was inexpedient and even politically foolish. A major critic early in the war, Hans Morgenthau, was actually one of the architects of the realpolitik upon which Washington based its policy.* Critics like Morgenthau argued that the United States should indeed establish its power *vis a vis* Chinese Communism but that Vietnam was not the place to do it. The small country was irrelevant to American security and a most unfavorable battlefield. China's interest in friendly neighbors was as justified as the United States' similar interest in the western hemisphere.

---

* *Realpolitik* refers to the idea that governmental policy should be based on the pragmatic realities of political and military power, not on ideology or morality.

While the peace movement generally used moral arguments, "establishment" opponents of the war continued this line of reasoning.

A similar dissent argued from the long Vietnamese hostility toward China that a Vietnam united under Ho Chi Minh would function toward China much as Tito's Yugoslavia functioned toward Soviet Russia. That is, though a united Vietnam would certainly be communist, it would be not satellite of its powerful neighbor. To such analysts, the tragedy of the American war was that the longer the United States remained in Vietnam, the more likely was North Vietnam to fall into China's debt and become in fact a client state.

A third political point of view was concerned with the effect of the war upon American policy and influence elsewhere in the world. In only a handful of nations did a majority of people approve American actions. The United States' reputation for fairness and goodwill in international dealings was indelibly stained, some protesters felt, by its unreasonable and brutal behavior in Vietnam. Japan and India, two nations the United States claimed to be protecting in Vietnam, both disapproved of the war. Relations with America's oldest friend, France, were hopelessly shattered at least in part by Vietnam. Developing nations looked warily on the United States lest they become the next object of intervention. The hopeful promise of *rapprochement* with the Soviet Union seemed to founder on the question of Vietnam alone. A United States with bloody hands seemed ludicrous and impotent when it counselled Israelis and Arabs on the virtues of peace.

Other opponents of the war emphasized its effects at home. American life, apparently so full of promise in 1960, seemed poisoned to them. The government lied so often that *credibility gap*—the expression of a general feeling that the Johnson Administration could not be trusted—became after *escalation* a frequent catch-phrase in political discussion. Television and the press, theoretically gadflies of government, were accused by the anti-war opposition of behaving like *Pravda* in their mouthing of Administration lines. Furthermore, American youth, according to psychologists, was becoming callous and insensitive as a result of the nightly violence on the television screen.

Domestic reform programs, sorely needed to rectify imbalances in American life and to stave off seasonal chaos in the country's sick cities, were shaved down or scrapped completely as the government pumped its treasury into the war effort. Financial experts warned that the bloated national war economy might end in disaster after the war, if not during it.* Taxes rose without compensating social services. Prices climbed throughout 1967. A larger and larger number of American workers seemed economically dependent on war.

Social critics observed that American politics were becoming dangerously polarized.† As the large anti-war movement lost its faith in the virtue of the American political system, another political extreme developed among those who could not understand how a tiny nation of Asians could wrestle the United

---

* See Marriner S. Eccles speech, *Dispatcher* (September 1, 1967), 5.

† *Protest from the Right*, another Insight Series book by Robert Rosenstone, deals with the extreme right wing in America.

States to the mat. With no conception of the nature of the new warfare, a fringe clamored for the simple solution of nuclear war. Opponents of the war charged that this fringe overlapped into the military and augured ill for the future of American democracy. The fact that the federal government itself approved repressive measures against dissenters drove many civil libertarians who otherwise might have supported the war into the movement calling for its end.

A few prominent military experts condemned the war. Some strategists said that the United States had concentrated a dangerously large part of its military resources in one unimportant country. By mid-1967 a half million men were committed to Vietnam and still managed only to hold their own. If, as the government claimed, one object of American intervention was to demonstrate the futility of the "war of national liberation," it was doing a poor job of it. The military lesson of Vietnam, strategists suggested, was that a rag-tag group of poorly armed and undernourished peasants with minimal outside aid could tie down a half million troops from the best-equipped and most powerful military force in the world. What would happen if, as seemed likely, similar wars broke out in Guatemala, Bolivia, the Congo, Brazil, or South Africa? Could the United States cope with each as it had coped (barely) with the Vietcong? If anything Vietnam vindicated the guerrilla theory that a war of national liberation exerted a power out of all proportion to its numbers and primitive technology.

Other military objectors to the war concentrated on the idea that the war was not winable by any standard. The United States was not "liberating" Vietnam as it had liberated Europe; it was fighting guerrillas in their homeland, and the bulk of the population was undeniably hostile. To expand the war to Cambodia and North Vietnam, the apparent trend of American policy in early 1968, would compound the same problem. To take the war to China would mean disaster, for even with nuclear weapons China's huge decentralized population could still not be subjugated. Did the United States wish to occupy its conquered territory indefinitely? The only alternative to such a lamentable form of victory was extermination of the population.

The Growth of a Radical Consensus

These arguments and others were developed, elaborated upon, and refined through the evolution of the anti-war movement in the sixties. But by 1967 the dominant point of view within the movement was the analysis of the most radical protesters. The crux of the war in Vietnam, the radicals argued, was not the matter of expediency or the peculiar brutality of its execution. The point was that the United States was fundamentally wrong. They were not interested in a compromise which would save face or protect American power. America was supporting a corrupt, reactionary government in Saigon while the National Liberation Front represented both the choice of the Vietnamese people and that country's best hope for the future. The United States should simply get out of Vietnam.

The American government could not be persuaded by reason or arguments of expediency and morality because the United States government, they felt, had become an imperialist power bent on the defense of the frontiers of its empire, not against Chinese expansionism but against an indigenous people.

In fact, they charged, American foreign policy was designed to protect not American interests or democratic interests but the interests of American capital. While our capitalists had few concrete investments in Vietnam before 1960, they had many in a score of other revolution-prone countries where, if the Vietcong won, revolutions might be expected wholesale. The government had won the support of the American people for its ventures through surreptitious escalation of the war, lies about its nature and progress, and resort to the "last refuge of scoundrels," irrational patriotism. In the words of a popular picket sign, "Big Firms Get Rich While GI's Die."

According to the growing anti-war consensus, then, the problem was not merely to effect an end to the war. Without a fundamental reorganization of American economy and society, the next Vietnam was only a matter of time. The problem was to effect a domestic revolution so that the life of the United States was not dependent on the exploitation of foreign peoples.

While radicals of this disposition were, with the pacifists, among the first opponents of the war, it was only after seven years that their argument began to influence the movement at large. Many individuals who first soured on the Vietnam policy because of its seeming inexpediency or brutality came through their frustration to delve more deeply into the causes of the war and they often adopted the radical idea. The potential effects of the Vietnamese War on the United States were numerous. One was that, if it did not end in nuclear disaster, a viable radical political movement might emerge in the United States.*

Vietnam: Vision of Hell (1967)

The Fellowship of Reconciliation

Pacifists see war as inherently brutal but, along with other humanitarians, they were particularly sickened by American prosecution of the war in Vietnam. No one attributed the atrocities of the war to any peculiar American penchant

---

* The amount of material published by the movement against the war in Vietnam is incredibly vast. The movement itself was large and comprised of dozens of independent groups, of which apparently few lacked access to at least a mimeograph machine. The quality of the matter varied from profound analysis to screeching absurdity. Criticisms of the war appeared in the editorial columns of the *New York Times* and on flyers handed out at supermarkets on a Saturday morning. These will someday provide the substance for an exhaustive study. The few presented here are by no means comprehensive. Several points of view are represented but they cannot begin to provide the reader with more than a taste of the literature of the protest.

for them; indeed many lamented that the war transfigured normally compassionate young men into brutes despite themselves. This was an army fighting
a people—that was why the American war was inevitably immoral. The imper-
sonality of modern military technology, moreover, made discrimination between
combatant and innocent impossible. A supersonic pilot merely pushed a button,
critics pointed out. They wondered if he would be able to pour burning gasoline
on women and children if he had to do it by hand.

This reading is an excerpt from a pamphlet describing the cruelties of the
war, entitled "They Are Our Brothers Whom We Help," printed by the Fellowship of Reconciliation.

"War is hell, by God, and this is one prime example," an American
officer told William Tuohy, the Saigon bureau chief of *Newsweek*. Tuohy
went on to describe "the problem": "fragmentation bombs sometimes
fall on defenseless peasants; artillery shells are fired at random into
the paddy fields. An appalling number of victims are women, children
and old men; some are participants but most are noncombatants."

The mechanics of the problem are in part suggested by a report
from Bernard Fall, Professor of International Relations at Howard
University, and a long-time observer of Vietnamese affairs. On a recent
trip to South Vietnam, he was permitted to fly as an observer with
an American attack group:

> Our "Skyraider" was loaded with 750-pound napalm bombs
> and 500-pound napalm bombs.... Our wing load carried 7,500
> pounds of high explosive anti-personnel bombs. We were in the
> lead plane going in....

> .   .   .   .

> There were probably between 1,000 and 1,500 people living in
> the fishing village we attacked. It is difficult to estimate how many
> were killed. It is equally difficult to judge if there actually were
> any Vietcong in the village, and if so, if any were killed....

The same type of tragedy is reported, though from ground level, by
a priest–victim as interviewed for *Paris-Match* by the anti-Communist
novelist, Jean Larteguy.

> "It began at 9 A.M.," Father Currien stated. "No one was in
> the village except for some women, children and old people, whom
> neither the Vietcong nor the regular troops thought to pick up as
> coolies.

> "I heard some planes. The first bomb fell on my church. There
> was nothing left to it. I ran for shelter to the presbytery, a wooden
> house adjoining the church. A second bomb crushed it and I was
> pinned under the beams. Children cried, women shrieked and the

wounded moaned. They were near me but I could not budge. Finally, some of the faithful who had been looking for me dragged me out. I made the women and children lie down under the flooring of the house. There we passed the entire night while those accursed planes hammered with rockets and bombs at my village."

.   .   .   .

The priest wept, and continued:
"I have seen my faithful burned up with napalm. I have seen the bodies of women and children blown to bits. I have seen all my villages razed. My God, it's not possible!"

Whether Fr. Currien's villages were in one of the "open bombing" sectors of Vietnam is not known. There are, however, constantly shifting areas of Vietnam in which pilots are authorized to bomb at will—villages, cattle, anything or anyone that moves. Pilots—for reasons of safety—are not permitted to land with their bomb loads.[1]

.   .   .   .

The War Against Rice

The war does not end with the destruction of suspect villages. In Vietnam, the crops too may be an enemy. The NLF must eat. According to government figures during the first six months of 1966, 59,000 acres of rice were destroyed. Presumably the figure for jungle defoliation is much higher. Program spokesmen have stated the effort will widen.

The problems caused by crop destruction were discussed in a June 29, 1966 issue of *The Christian Century*, written by Dr. Victor Sidel (Chief of Preventive Medicine at Massachusetts General Hospital, Boston, and Associate in Preventive Medicine at the Harvard Medical School) and Dr. Jean Mayer (Professor of Nutrition at Harvard):

The aim is, of course, to starve the Viet Cong. . . . In essence this aim is similar to that of every food blockade.

As a nutritionist who has seen famines on three continents, one of them Asia, and as a physician with a basic interest in preventive medicine, we can say flatly that there has never been a famine or a food shortage—whatever might have been its cause— which has not first and overwhelmingly affected the small children.

.   .   .   .

The mortality picture is clear. Death from starvation occurs first and overwhelmingly in small children, then in older children and in the elderly. Adolescents are more likely to survive, though

---

[1] Bernard B. Fall "Vietnam Album," *Ramparts* (December, 1965).

they are most susceptible to tuberculosis. Pregnant women not infrequently abort; lactating mothers invariably cease to produce milk and the babies die. Adult men are far less affected.

If the efforts toward crop destruction are in fact growing and if the techniques have been worked out, it seems that very soon a much larger area could be destroyed and famine could become widespread.

.   .   .   .

The Wounded and Dying

Despite extraordinary efforts by doctor–volunteers from many nations, hospital care is pathetically inadequate to the needs. Many of the more seriously wounded are not even able to get to the provincial hospitals, it is reported, as there are no ambulances. Some of the victims are brought in by helicopter, but not in the cases of simple air destruction of a village or region.

Some indication of the situation is provided by a report from Terre des Hommes, a Swiss agency caring for child war victims. The author is a surgeon:

Only one [of the four hospitals we visited] seems to operate normally. The three others show the frightening spectacle of immense distress, to the extent that one finds children burned from head to foot who are treated only with vaseline, because of the lack of (a) ointment for burns, (b) cotton, (c) gauze, (d) personnel. In places with the atmosphere of slaughter houses for people, where flies circulate freely on children who have been skinned alive, there are no facilities for hygiene, no fans and no air conditioning.

Two Dutch doctors, one a plastic surgeon, the other an intern, made the following report to the Dutch press upon returning from Vietnam:

It is indescribable. Thousands of people suffering from untended burns arrive from the interior of the country. Nobody takes care of these unfortunate people because no one seems to know what could be done. In Vietnam one encounters all the forms of infectious diseases and their complications. Every tenth Vietnamese suffers from tuberculosis. Numerous types of sickness are not treated. There is an unimaginable number of persons suffering from war wounds. The few existing hospitals are overflowing with patients. It is not rare for three persons to share the same bed. There are practically no nurses. Most people are tended by members of their own family, who usually sleep in the hospital itself, under the bed or next to it, anywhere they can find room. No efficient treatment of burns is used.

Martha Gellhorn, an American war correspondent who has covered wars in Spain, Finland, China, England, Italy, France, Germany, and Java, describes one Vietnamese hospital in a recent series for England's *Guardian:*

> The Qui Nhon provincial hospital is crowded to bursting with wounded peasants, men, women and children of all ages, none of whom would be alive were it not for the New Zealand surgical teams which have served in this hospital since 1963.
>
> The people answer quietly, emotion shows only in their eyes. The old are pitiful in their bewilderment, the adults seem locked in an aloof resignation, the children's ward is unbearable. No one protests or complains. We big, overfed white people will never know what they feel.
>
> A boy of 15 sat on his cot with both legs in plaster casts. He and his little brother had gone to the beach to mend nets; a Vietnamese patrol boat saw them and opened up with machine gun fire; his little brother was killed. . . .
>
> The children do not cry out in pain; if they make any sound it is a soft moaning; they twist their wounded bodies in silence. In the cot by the door is a child burned by napalm. He is seven years old, the size of a four-year-old of ours. His face and back and bottom are burned. A little piece of something like cheesecloth covers his body; it seems that any weight would be intolerable, but so is air. His hand is burned, stretched out like a starfish; the napalmed skin on the little body looks like bloodied hardened meat in the butcher's shop. ("We always get the napalm cases in batches," the doctor has said. And there's white phosphorus too, worse because it goes on gnawing at flesh like rat's teeth, gnawing to the bone.) An old man nearly blind with a cataract, was tending this burned child, his grandson. The napalm bombs fell a week ago [September, 1966] on their hamlet; he carried the child to the nearest town and they were flown here by helicopter. The child cried with pain all that week but today he is better, he is not crying, only twisting his body to try to find some way to lie that does not hurt him. . . .

.   .   .   .

The Orphans

"They bring us so many, many," a nun in a Saigon orphanage said. "The father is killed in the war, the woman has four children, seven children, she is too poor. The mothers cry when they give us their children. They cry very much."

And there are those other children with no mother, no father, no one at all.

No one knows how many orphans there are in Vietnam. Officially, there are 80,000 registered in the South. That is, there are 80,000 in the institutions, the home of last resort. How many more have been absorbed by uncles, cousins, or surviving neighbors can only be guessed.

The Ministry of Social Welfare predicts 2,000 more orphans each month.

Martha Gellhorn interviewed one of the nuns—Sister Jeanne—Superior of one of Saigon's ten orphanages for children.

Each one of the orphans is allotted twelve piastres a day by the government, about enough for a small bowl of cooked rice or a gallon of water. The rest Sister Jeanne must beg. Programs for occupational therapy, medical care and education cannot even be considered.

> Sister Jeanne talked encouragingly in Vietnamese to a girl of about 16 [Miss Gellhorn reported] and slowly, as if her back were broken, the girl tried to raise herself to a sitting position. "Hysterical paralysis," Sister Jeanne said. "Her mother was killed in their hamlet, bombs; and the girl was left alone with her father. It is curious for only two to remain in a Vietnamese family. Then one morning the girl woke and her father was dead; I don't know how. She became completely paralyzed at once, but she moves a little more each day."
>
> Farther down the long room, a middle-aged woman babbled and laughed, and a little girl of 6 or 7 tumbled over her head. She smiled at this cheerful pair and said: "They have lost their reason, poor things. They are harmless and happier here; I do not want to send them to the horrible government lunatic asylum. Many women have gone mad from their sufferings; children too."

Military Opposition to the War (1966–1967)

The inclusiveness of the anti-war movement was demonstrated by the number of high military men who attacked the war. Their arguments ranged from that of General James Gavin, who called it militarily preposterous, to the moralistic position of the former commandant of the Marine Corps, General David M. Shoup. One of the most dramatic military dissents was that of Brigadier General Robert L. Hughes, U.S. Army Reserve, at a 1967 Memorial Day meeting on the state capitol grounds at Madison, Wisconsin. "The true significance of the day is most poignant to those who have suffered the loss of a loved one in the present conflict in Vietnam," Hughes began in standard fashion. These loved ones, he then said, had "died in support of an unstable foreign government that is maintained only by the strength of the United States." He called the Saigon government a clique of "morally corrupt leaders who adhere to a warlord philosophy" and concluded to the amazed audience: "This is one hell of a war to be fighting. We must disengage from this tragic war. It is the only one in which we have committed troops without first being aggressed against."

These statements were excerpted and widely distributed by several anti-war organizations including Clergy and Laymen Concerned About Vietnam, and Veterans for Peace.

GENERAL DAVID M. SHOUP, *former Commandant of the U.S. Marine Corps;* speaking at the tenth Annual Junior College World Affairs Day, Pierce College, Los Angeles, May 14, 1966:

You read, you're televised to, you're radioed to, you're preached to, that it is necessary that we have our armed forces fight, get killed and maimed, and kill and maim other human beings including women and children because now is the time we must stop some kind of unwanted ideology from creeping up on this nation. The place we chose to do this is 8,000 miles away with water in between. . . .

The reasons fed to us are too shallow and narrow for students, as well as other citizens. Especially so, when you realize that what is happening, no matter how carefully and slowly the military escalation has progressed, may be projecting us toward world catastrophe. Surely, it is confusing. . . .

I want to tell you, I don't think the whole of Southeast Asia, as related to the present and future safety and freedom of the people of this country, is worth the life or limb of a single American. . . .

I believe that if we had and would keep our dirty, bloody, dollar-crooked fingers out of the business of these nations so full of depressed, exploited people, they will arrive at a solution of their own. That they design and want. That they fight and work for. And if unfortunately their revolution must be of a violent type because the 'haves' refuse to share with the 'have-nots' by any peaceful method, at least what they get will be their own, and not the American style, which they don't want and above all don't want crammed down their throats by Americans.

LT. GENERAL JAMES GAVIN; testifying before the U.S. Senate Committee on Foreign Relations, February 21, 1967:

[The use of] bombing attacks intended to achieve psychological impact through the killing of noncombatants is unquestionably wrong.

Likewise the attack of targets near areas highly populated by civilians where civilians are likely to be casualities, is also militarily as well as morally wrong. . . .

I believe that we can negotiate with Hanoi and with the National Liberation Front confident that a free, neutral and independent Vietnam can be established, with guarantees of stability from an international body.

BRIG. GENERAL HUGH B. HESTER; writing to Veterans for Peace in Vietnam, May 8, 1967:

I opposed U.S. involvement in Indochina in 1954, as did General Ridgeway, then Chief of Staff of the U.S. Army. Both of us feared this would involve U.S. ground forces in the jungles and swamps of Asia against the almost limitless Asian masses.

I have opposed every increase in that involvement since. I oppose the Vietnamese War now, not only because it is being waged in violation of the UN Charter, but also because it is in violation of the basic interests of the American people. The Vietnam War is not a war of self-defense or even of general self-interest. It is a war in the profit interests of only a very few.

REAR ADMIRAL ARNOLD E. TRUE; writing to the editor of the *Palo Alto* (Calif.) *Times*, March 3, 1966:

We can end the Vietnam fiasco without dishonor by (1) dealing with the Vietcong as a major party to the war, (2) implementing the Geneva Accords, (3) withdrawing our troops, and (4) letting the Vietnamese settle their own problems. . . .

General Ky is naturally willing to fight to the last American soldier and the last American dollar. It is about time that Americans should make their own decisions and stop blabbing about "commitments" and saying "it is up to Hanoi."

GENERAL MATTHEW B. RIDGEWAY. *U.S. Commander in Chief in the Far East*, 1951–1952; *U.S. Army Chief of Staff*, 1953–1955; writing in *Look Magazine*, April 5, 1967:

It is my firm belief that there is nothing in the present situation or in our code that requires us to bomb a small Asian nation back into the stone age.

A Faked Class B Movie (1965)

I. F. Stone

The most persistent and comprehensive journalistic critic of the Vietnamese intervention was I. F. Stone. In his newsletter, *I. F. Stone's Weekly*, Stone ranged from American atrocities in Vietnam to the effects of the war at home. Stone was most telling when he dissected government rationalizations for the war, picking apart their contradictions until little remained.

Stone also scored several scoops on the war. His report on the Tonkin Gulf Incident (an alleged North Vietnamese attack on American naval vessels which President Johnson used to secure congressional *carte blanche* for his prosecution of the war) included the observation that the President had prepared his resolution long before and waited only for some pretext to send it to Congress. Stone also wondered about the validity of the incident, uncovering evidence which impugned the President's account. The mass media ignored Stone's observations when he made them, publicizing them two years later as if they were freshly-discovered insights. Stone also scooped the mass media by over a year with his analyses of how the United States sabotaged various peace feelers from the NLF and North Vietnamese while the government maintained at home that the enemy did not wish to negotiate.

"It's Been a Faked Class B Movie from the Beginning." from the *Weekly* for January 25, 1965, focusses on the government's distortions of the situation.

Associated Press correspondent Peter Arnett drove south of Saigon January 14 to check reports of a battle and found U.S. Information Officers staging fake war scenes for a propaganda film. "We don't want to show cruel things like bodies," an information officer in charge explained, "and we will avoid references to tanks, fighter aircraft, and artillery. This is a people-to-people film. . . ." When the story broke, the film was, of course, disavowed by USIA Director Carl T. Rowan. Only those with short memories will be taken in by the disavowal. The Vietnamese war, as far as the information given the American people is concerned, has been a faked class B movie from the beginning. The Moss subcommittee of the House two years ago protested the information practices of the State Department on Vietnam. It called attention to a speech by Mr. Rowan in which he spoke of the public's "right *not* to know in a period of undeclared war." Even this cynical statement misstated the facts. What is involved is not just "the right *not* to know" but the government's right to deceive. President Kennedy himself tried at one point to get a *New York Times* man transferred from Vietnam because he was reporting the war too independently for the government's taste.

Doctoring the Record

Every agency of government is drawn into this campaign of deception. The Senate Foreign Relations Committee last week put out what purported to be an objective volume of "background information" on the war in Vietnam. It is supposed to be a compilation of the important official statements. But the record is tailored. The fullest official reports to the public on the war were the Blue Book the State Department issued in the fall of 1961 to explain Kennedy's decision to intervene; Secretary Rusk's speech to the Economic Club in New York April 22, 1963; and Secretary McNamara's speech to the National Security Industrial Association (an arms lobby mouthpiece) on March 26 of last year. All three pictured South Vietnam under Diem as a model of progress and democracy, an "economic miracle" comparable to West Germany (no less!), a land of such contented people (land reform, educational expansion) that the Communists in desperation resorted to invasion as their only hope of reunifying the country. This notion that guerrilla war can successfully be carried on in a prosperous country, amid a happy people, is so preposterous that even a public as doped-up as ours could no longer be expected to take it seriously. In the Foreign Relations handbook not a scrap remains of the two-volume Blue Book. Rusk's speech has disappeared altogether. Discreet editorial scissors have cut out of McNamara's speech the whole opening section with its glowing picture of what McNamara called the Vietnamese "success story." Why should the Foreign Relations Committee, which is supposed to provide some check on the State Department, help to hide this record of deception?

Even Senators Uninformed

Even members of Congress, who get private briefings, show an extraordinary ignorance of what has been going on. McGovern of South Dakota made a good speech in the Senate, January 15. It echoed De Gaulle's suggestion that the war be ended by negotiating the neutralization of the area. McGovern opposed expansion of the war. "Attacks on North Vietnam," he said, "will not seriously weaken guerrilla fighters a thousand miles away, fighters who depend for 80 per cent of their weapons on captured U.S. equipment and for food on a sympathetic local peasantry." But then he went on to make a suggestion which shows how little senators are told. He said that "the most practical way" to put pressure on North Vietnam was "quietly through infiltration and subversion by South Vietnamese units" into the North with the aim not of "military victory" but of "bringing Ho Chi Minh to the negotiating table."

This is doubly ludricrous. Ho Chi Minh has been trying to get to the bargaining table for two years. The problem is to get the United States to the bargaining table. He has made clear his readiness to accept a neutralized independent South Vietnam in return for peace and resumption of North–South trade. The idea of using commando raids on the North for "infiltration and subversion" which McGovern recommends is not new. There is evidence that such raiding operations were begun ten years ago when our leading counter-guerilla expert, Gen. Lansdale, was Diem's military adviser. These operations represent a major political and military defeat. The infiltrees have never succeeded in sparking local anti-Communist guerrilla uprisings. Richard Dudman of the *St. Louis Post–Dispatch* reported a year ago (February 26, 1964) that officials were disillusioned about infiltrating the North. "Although it is not generally known," Mr. Dudman wrote, "special South Vietnamese troops already have been parachuted into North Vietnam on missions of espionage and sabotage. They have vanished."

How We Broke the Geneva Pact

These cloak-and-dagger activities, which began five years before fighting broke out in the South, were a violation by the United States of the Geneva agreement of 1954. Though we did not sign the agreement, we pledged ourselves not to upset neutralization of the area by force. The training and supply of those early commando raids violated that pledge. So did our Progress Evaluation Office in Laos, a disguised military mission of U.S. officers in civilian clothes who took over control of the armed forces in Laos in the same period. They twice engineered the overthrow of its neutralist Prime Minister Souvanna Phouma and are still at it.

It is a pity Chairman Fulbright of Senate Foreign Relations does not take time off from retailing safe liberal generalities about easily discernible "myths" and use his committee to give the U.S. public a thorough investigation of what is going on. We went to the conference table in Geneva in 1962 to save Laos from being completely taken over by the left when our rightist military proteges faced collapse. The price was an agreement to neutralize the country and to establish a coalition government of the three factions under Souvanna Phouma. The aerial bombardment of Laos now coming to public knowledge with the loss of more planes to enemy action was made possible by the overthrow of Souvanna Phouma for the third time last April. Though he was restored, the conditions were such as to make him and the neutralists prisoners of the right. With the coalition destroyed, the way was clear to escalate the war by having the Laotian government invite the U.S. to send its planes into Laos for "reconnaisance." This violated the promises made at Geneva in 1962. Laos offers an ideal way to satisfy the demand for escalation without direct attacks on North Vietnam or China. The recent bombings, notably that on the bridge at Ban Ban, have been overplayed in the U.S. press. Our public, brought up on movies about the bridge across the River Kwai, pictures Ban Ban as a jugular attack. But this bridge is not anywhere near that legendary Ho Chi Minh supply trail to South Vietnam, and bridges are of little importance anyway in small scale guerrilla fighting. This is another phony "movie" about the war.

The Futility of Vietnam (1967)

Walter Lippmann

Military strategists and political commentators with a knowledge of military affairs attempted to point out that superiority of numbers and incomparable technological superiority was not sufficient to win the war in Vietnam. It was suggested that the escalation of the war would never have occurred had American military leaders recognized that increasing the size of the American effort was irrelevant to the National Liberation Front's type of war. The dean of American political columnists, Walter Lippmann, expressed this view in his Washington Post Syndicate column for December 10, 1967, which is reprinted here by permission.

Nothing is more puzzling to Americans than that the most powerful nation on earth is taking so long to subdue a poor little country like North Vietnam. According to conventional wisdom, the enemy should have recognized long ago that the odds against him are overpowering and he should have given up. He has not done so as yet, and, if he is going to do it, he is taking a long time about it.

What is more, it begins to appear that even if he surrendered there would probably be no more than a temporary truce before guerrilla fighting broke out again. As a matter of fact, it is very difficult even to imagine how this war can end. Even if Hanoi and Haiphong were bombed back to the Stone Age and Ho Chi Minh signed an unconditional surrender on an American aircraft carrier, there would be peace and Saigon and General Westmoreland would still have to remain on the alert.

The war, it would seem, is unwinnable in a much deeper sense than is commonly realized. It is not that our forces cannot defeat the enemy's forces in battle. It is that the battles they fight cannot decide the war. It is unwinnable in the sense that a horde of elephants cannot win a struggle with a swarm of mosquitoes, not because the mosquitoes are too brave or too fanatic, but because mosquitoes do not surrender to elephants. No mosquito can surrender all the mosquitoes that can be bred in the marsh and no government or committee or general can surrender the revolutionary peasantry of the Asian continent.

What we are witnessing is not a conflict between two military forces of different sizes, but of two military forces that are different in kind. The conflict is between two quite different military systems. One consists of a highly centralized organization using the deadliest weapons; the other consists of endlessly decentralized swarms of guerrilla fighters and terrorists.

North Vietnam is testing, so we are often told, whether "wars of national liberation" can succeed. That is true. It is testing whether guerrilla fighters with a continent behind them and an inexhaustible horde of discontented people can be subdued by military forces developed and organized to fight against equally organized powers with equally advanced weapons. Our most bewildering and perhaps our most significant experience in the Vietnamese war has been that the kind of military force which brought down Japan and Germany does not bring down Ho Chi Minh and the Vietcong.

The fact that although we are able to destroy the enemy's country we are not able to win the war is something new in our experience of warfare. We are up against something which is different in kind from anything that West Point and Annapolis anticipated. We defeated Japan and the victory endured in the sense Japan rose again and prospered and we are hoping to make it our ally. But if we could dictate peace in Hanoi after the surrender of Ho Chi Minh, it would be only a question of time before the anti-Communist and pro-American regime we had set up in South Vietnam would be undermined and would crumble.

In the long run, perhaps the most important consequence of the present war in Vietnam will be the demonstration that the strongest military power in history cannot by the use of its superior firepower impose its will on a distant people. The elephants can kill every mosquito they can trample upon. But in the marshes, the swarms of mosquitoes are constantly renewed.

I have read not all but a good many of the books about modern military technology—both those dealing with big weapons and with guerilla fighting. I have not seen anything which describes how the big and little technologies of war fail to come to a decisive confrontation, how they are like ships which brush against each other in the night without colliding.

Vietnam is No Mistake (1967)

John McDermott

In this essay, from the *Nation* for February 13, 1967, John McDermott examines three common ideas about American intervention in Vietnam. His analysis is written for those already critical of the war. It is a radical's document, for McDermott sees the war neither as an aberration in American foreign policy nor as a blunder. The war, he says, is part of a rational calculated policy authored by men whom, by implication, must be removed from power; they cannot be persuaded to change.

That the *Nation* should in this instance serve as a sort of internal organ of the anti-war movement and that John McDermott should write a radical analysis of the war is dramatic evidence of the radicalization of liberal thinking. The *Nation* is the country's oldest liberal journal; it has always regarded itself as within the mainstream of American politics. McDermott was a professor of philosophy who, by his own account, was quite conventional politically before Vietnam. He is presently associate editor of *Viet-Report*, a journal of Vietnamese affairs.

Three current myths, widely held even among critics of the war in Vietnam, vitiate any effort to build popular support for new and more moderate foreign policies. The first myth holds that the continual escalation of the war by the Johnson Administration stems from the fundamental misconception that the Vietnamese crisis originated outside the South, that is, in Hanoi or, possibly, Peking. Because of this misconception, the myth concludes, events themselves will frustrate the policy, educate the policy makers and thus create, ultimately, the basis for an end to the war. Myth number two, which frequently shares billing with the first, portrays American foreign policy as containment. In this view, our policy is a minimal one, aimed merely at containing China (or communism or whatever) until Peking gives up its expansionist propensities and learns to live in peace and harmony with the rest of the world. The third myth is the most dangerous of all. It asserts that United States foreign policy can and must be understood as an attempt to maintain a balance of power with the Communist world.

None of these is even faintly true. Contrary to myth number one, and as press reports amply demonstrate, responsible United States policy makers, far from being chagrined by the growing folly of the war, are delighted at what they consider its outstanding success to date. As for myth number two, American policy is not aimed at containing the power of China, of the Soviet Union, of the various Communist movements; it aims instead at crippling that power, at rolling it back and, where possible, destroying it. And the third myth invokes a balance of power that does not, and cannot, exist in the world today. America has no power rival in any part of the world. By contrast, the Soviet Union is at best a regional power and, in Washington's estimate, a second-line power at that.

We should not be surprised that Washington is happy with the progress of the Vietnamese war. Although its war policies have been partially rebuked by the American electorate and wholly stalemated by the Vietnamese enemy, the Administration has three very good reasons for celebration.

Notwithstanding the oft-voiced expectations of the critics that escalation of the war would drive China and the Soviet Union into each other's arms, the Vietnamese crisis has aggravated their differences almost to the breaking point. Since it is a major aim of Administration policy to keep its enemies divided, the Vietnamese war has on this count been an exemplary success.

Moscow's inability to aid its beleaguered ally in Hanoi other than by modest shipments of arms and munitions has taught the East European states how much Soviet protection is worth. Accordingly, the escalation, again refuting the critics, has contributed to loosening still further Soviet influence in eastern Europe.

By polarizing Communist and non-Communist positions in the Far East, escalation has led to a stiffening of will on the part of the non-Communists, especially in Indonesia, Singapore and Malaysia. Similarly, the escalation has helped foster internal convulsions in China, with the result that the Japanese and Korean Communist Parties have defected from the Maoist "line." U.S. policy in Vietnam has thus contributed to the increasing isolation of China in the Far East.

The first point is true and, purely as policy, it is also unexceptionable. Any foreign office placed in the position of Mr. Rusk's State Department would try to divide the Soviet Union and China. But pressing the question further begins to reveal what is peculiar about U.S. policy in this instance. One notes immediately that it has little to do with Vietnam itself. There is good reason to believe that policy makers in Washington, whatever their views may have been in the past, now realize that the Vietnamese war stems from long-term disputes among various Vietnamese political factions, and that the role of China, as of the international Communist movements, has been distinctly ancillary. More even than that, I am persuaded that Administration leaders know how to negotiate an end to the war on relatively favorable terms, and may even do so well prior to the 1968 elections. First, however, they want to exploit still further the differences between Moscow and Peking, and this prescribes that the war continue. We are confronted here with great-power politics of the most conventional—and ruthless—kind. The Administration is quite consciously destroying Vietnam and its people in order to gain a marginal advantage elsewhere. This is a rational choice, not a mistake or a miscalculation.

The significance of this choice should be dwelt upon. Even granting, for argument's sake, the desirability of a Soviet–Chinese split, we must ask why Administration leaders use war to accomplish it. Both the Soviets and the Chinese have made it known that they strongly desire foreign credits as well as increased trade. In addition, China must import much of its grain supply. A clever trade policy on Washington's part, forcing the Soviets and Chinese to compete with each other for substantial trade advantages, would likely exacerbate their relations quite as much as a war in Vietnam. Supposing this trade strategy effective, the United States would have not one enemy, China, or two, China and Russia, but none, while its major rivals would still be divided. But Washington has not chosen this course. Why?

The answer to this question is to be found in an analysis of myth number two—that is, in what poses as a policy of containment. The Administration is not trying to contain China and the Soviet Union; it is trying to reduce them further to the status of second-line powers. Holding the Soviet case in abeyance for the moment, consider China. How can one speak of the need to contain China when in fact it is not expanding? Two critical examples demonstrate the truth of this assertion.

In 1954, both North Korea and North Vietnam could reasonably be considered Chinese satellites. China had paid dearly for this influence: it fought a major conventional war in Korea, and only narrowly avoided a nuclear attack in 1953 for its efforts there; it risked a similar attack a year later as a result of its assistance to the Vietminh. The strategic location of these small nations on China's sensitive borders and their inflammable rivalries with American-supported South Korea and

South Vietnam, respectively, should have guaranteed that an "expansionist" Chinese foreign office, still more its "aggressive" Communist Party, would maintain them as puppets. Nothing like that happened. Both Pyongyang and Hanoi have long since gravitated out of the Chinese orbit. Both have long pursued independent foreign policies; in both, the Communist Parties have long since been able to pick and choose among the competing views of the Communist world.

China has not been expanding—not against Japan, not against Burma and Pakistan, not even against India (and, since the late fifties, not even against Quemoy). Shrouded in truculent rhetoric, Peking's foreign policies have shown a basically moderate—even isolationist—character. But the United States has not been satisfied. Secretary Rusk and his associates want not a static Chinese international position but a declining one. They tell us this themselves when they point with satisfaction to China's growing isolation and offer it as one of the reasons to be satisfied by the course of the Vietnamese war.

A similar analysis may be made of Russia and the East European situation. Again, by their own testimony, American officials are not satisfied merely with the thaw in eastern Europe, which was already far advanced before Soviet weaknesses were exposed in Vietnam. The war in Vietnam is a good war, in their eyes, because it exposes Soviet military weaknesses *vis a vis* the United States, and thereby encourages the East European states to make separate arrangements with Washington or its chief ally in Europe, West Germany. The Administration probably assigns no very high priority to this objective, certainly not the priority given to rolling back Chinese influence in Asia. Nonetheless, one must recognize here a milder form of the old *roll-back-the-iron-curtain* policy that John Foster Dulles tried to pursue until the development of Soviet ICBM's in 1957 forced the Eisenhower Administration to seek a detente.

The Johnson Administration, under its chief foreign policy theorist, Walt Whitman Rostow, has developed a new rollback policy, less crude and less bombastic than that of Secretary Dulles, but still a rollback policy and not less dangerous for being more oblique. Administration officials would deny the charge if made in these words. But, at the operating level, they accept as concrete foreign policy values, worth our bitter sacrifices in Vietnam, a systematic rollback of Soviet and, especially, Chinese influence.

That is the chief significance of the policies of counter-insurgency which grew out of the fall of Batista in Cuba in the late fifties, and which have gained such impetus from the Vietnamese war. In W. W. Rostow's still-classic presentation of the objectives of military counter-

insurgency operations, given at Fort Bragg in 1961, he strongly em-
phasizes that a successful counter-insurgency strategy must begin long
before native dissidents are ready for—or even thinking of—guerrilla
warfare. Why then mount military operations against them? In
Rostow's view, the answer is very simple. Native dissidents represent,
at the very least, a latent Soviet or Chinese influence. Because of this,
and for no other reason in Rostow's view, they must be destroyed.
Counter-insurgency policy demands that America first must *expand* its
influence in the underdeveloped world and, second, that it must use
that influence to mount an *offensive* against Moscow's or Peking's
"allies" there. From this standpoint it is not a strategy of containment
(or of peaceful coexistence) since its defined objective is the diminution
of Sino-Soviet influence by military means. In short, the logic of
counter-insurgency has the logic of rollback built right in.

This brings up the third and critical myth, the myth that American
policy is to be understood within the framework of conventional
balance-of-power analysis. There is no balance of power in the world
and perhaps never in modern history has the world been so distant
from one. American power—military, economic, technical, political—
stands at heights beyond the reach not only of its enemies separately
but of the whole world together. Certainly the statement is noncon-
troversial if we exclude the Soviet Union. But what of the Soviets?
Have they not the power to deter America in the international arena?
To understand the answer to this question one must turn to one of
the great disasters of our era, President Kennedy's victory in the
Cuban missile crisis.

It is no quarrel with the necessity of President Kennedy's actions
to call his victory a disaster. Yet it was in November, 1962, that the
seeds of the rollback policy were sown. Ever since Hiroshima, secre-
taries of Defense (as well as presidents) have recited the familiar
litany of America's destructive power—a power, they claimed, which
dwarfed that of the Soviet Union and its allies. Until 1957, American
officials really believed in the predominance of our power; accordingly,
Dulles, like Acheson before him, could toy with the idea of a rollback
policy. With the advent of the Soviet ICBM in 1957 the power equation
seemed to change, and for several years there was serious concern in
Washington, evidenced by military sniping at President Eisenhower,
and culminating in the missile-gap controversy, that we had no such
advantage over the Soviets. When President Kennedy won office on a
pledge to restore American power in the world we should have taken
that pledge seriously. J.F.K. immediately added $6.5 billion to
Eisenhower's last military budget. Later, his own first military (and

space) budget exceeded Eisenhower's last by almost 50 per cent. But in spite of the impressive military build-up (unmatched by the Soviets) these fantastic expenditures represented, the Kennedy Administration seemed at first unaware that it had broken through into a military position which promised relative freedom of action in the world. But continued official belief in the *balance of terror* ended with the Cuban missile crisis. As Washington understood the result, the Soviets backed down. Faced with the prospect of testing the power implicit in the Kennedy rearmament program (which was not even at that time fully completed), Moscow turned away. It is not necessary to argue here whether or not this was indeed the significance of what happened. The important point is that Washington so interpreted it, and still does.

President Kennedy's victory in the Cuban missile crisis was a disaster because it persuaded high government figures that we had no serious rival, that when push came to shove, there was only one international superpower. Russian core interests did not extend to war over Cuba; the Soviet Union was only a regional power. Thus it followed that, provided Russia's regional interests were not directly threatened, the United States had a free hand elsewhere. It is now evident that *elsewhere* included North Vietnam. Was it an accident of timing that the Administration began bombing North Vietnam while Premier Kosygin was visiting Hanoi? Though our information on the attack is as yet incomplete, it may well have been intended as a sharp reminder to the Russians that they had neither the means nor the interest to involve themselves in a major conflict with the United States in the Far East. The Johnson Administration has learned the lesson of 1962 only too well. The bombing J.F.K. was afraid to risk in Cuba in 1962, L.B.J. may risk with impunity in North Vietnam today.

To analyze our policies in Vietnam and elsewhere is also to diagnose their source and thereby to suggest, if only implicitly, the counter-responses which are appropriate. Those who accept the three myths are inevitably placed in a position of arguing that in some fundamental sense only stupidity, ignorance—for some, neurosis—stand between current policy and a better, somewhat more humane and peaceful future. To accept such a conclusion is to be arrogant, abusive, un-historical, and, worse, ineffectual. The plain fact is that our current policy is led by able and determined men with coherent—if disagreeable —conceptions of the vast opportunities open to America's unchecked power, and the conscious will to use arbitrary force to achieve their ends. Accordingly, the appropriate response is not to educate them, enlighten them, psychoanalyze them, or even abuse them. Those who oppose them must begin instead to devise serious strategies for replacing them and, more important, the institutions and doctrines which have shaped them. These, the real villians of the piece, include bipartisan foreign policy, executive supremacy in foreign affairs, Congressional generosity to Defense and Space, the imperial mechanisms of foreign aid, the militarism of our civilian leadership, the doctrine of America's special responsibility for world leadership. It will be difficult to carry out a dramatic change in all those areas, but that program offers the only realistic alternative to the thirty-year series of "little wars" which Secretary McNamara, the Bundys, and the Rostows so willfully predict.